Irish
Renaissance
Annual I

Editorial Board

Manuscripts submitted should follow the *Chicago Manual of Style* in form and documentation. We expect that the *Irish Renaissance Annual* will appear every year in the spring.Contributions and inquiries should be addressed to Zack Bowen, the *Irish Renaissance Annual,* Department of English, University of Delaware, Newark, DE 19711.

The *Irish Renaissance Annual* is published by the University of Delaware Press through Associated University Presses.

Irish Renaissance Annual I

Edited by Zack Bowen

Newark
University of Delaware Press
London and Toronto: Associated University Presses

Associated University Presses, Inc.
Cranbury, New Jersey 08512

Associated University Presses
Magdalen House
136-148 Tooley Street
London SE1 2TT, England

Associated University Presses
Toronto M5E 1A7, Canada

ISSN 0-193-9777

1980
(Volume I, Number 1)

Contents

Notes on Contributors

MAURICE BEEBE, Professor of English at Temple University, started *Modern Fiction Studies* in 1955 and now edits *Journal of Modern Literature*. His many publications include *Ivory Towers and Sacred Founts: The Artist as Hero in Fiction from Goethe to Joyce* (1964) as well as critical casebooks, essays, reviews, and bibliographies. He is presently at work on a guide to the Age of Modernism.

JOHN COOKE is Assistant Professor of English and Drama at Le Moyne College where he teaches modern drama, Shakespeare, and acting and directing.

WAYNE HALL is currently Charles Phelps Taft Postdoctoral Fellow at the University of Cincinnati. His publications include a translation of the work of Werner Link for the Institute of German Studies at Indiana University and several essays in *Éire-Ireland*.

BRYANT E. HOFFMAN is Associate Professor of English at Colby-Sawyer College. His publications include essays in the *Literary Review* and the *Renaissance Quarterly*.

JAMES H. MATTHEWS is Associate Professor of Literature at Eckerd College. His *Frank O'Connor* appeared in the Bucknell Irish Writer series. He has published numerous articles in such journals as *Éire-Ireland*, the *Sewanee Review*, the *James Joyce Quarterly* and the *Journal of Irish Literature*. The essay in this volume is part of a full length biography of O'Connor, which Matthews is now completing.

ANTHONY T. MCCRANN is Assistant Professor of English at Daido Institute of Technology in Nagoya, Japan. He taught previously at Oregon College of Education and the University of Oregon.

THOMAS J. MORRISSEY is Assistant Professor of English and director of the writing skills program at the State University of New York College at Plattsburg. He has published several articles on both English and American literature.

FRITZ SENN lives near Zurich, Switzerland, and is an occasional Visiting Professor in the United States (Indiana University, SUNY Buffalo, Ohio State University, University of Hawaii, University of Delaware). He has been an editor of *A Wake Newslitter* and the *James Joyce Quarterly* since their beginning. He is a trustee (and since 1977 President) of the James Joyce Foundation. He has lectured widely and written numerous books, essays, and articles on Joyce.

Editor's Foreword

The *Irish Renaissance Annual* seeks to provide a forum for scholarship and criticism about modern Irish writers as well as essays devoted to relationships between literature and the other arts. Our intention in concentrating on literary scholarship is to supplement such general purpose journals as *Éire-Ireland* and *Anglo-Irish Studies,* publishers of creative works such as the *Journal of Irish Literature* and review periodicals such as the *American Committee for Irish Studies Newsletter.* The original intent of the journal was to publish material connected with the Rebellion of 1916 and Irish independence. The response to our call for manuscripts has been gratifying and continuing, but as so many of the clearly superior essays received for this first number touched only peripherally upon political matters, we have decided to be more flexible in our editorial policy, and will publish material even if only tentatively connected with the Rebellion. While we still intend to give preference to articles concerning 1916 and independence, we will entertain manuscripts on any aspect of modern Irish literature. As might be expected, there was a predominance of manuscripts on the giants—Yeats and Joyce—and since we are committed to a policy of publishing those essays most deserving, from year to year there may occasionally seem to be some imbalance. However, the studies of O'Connor, Moore, Synge, and Fitzmaurice appearing in this first volume, will, I think, testify to our commitment to all distinguished Irish literary writers.

Similarly, we have selected articles with diverse critical

approaches. The first three articles in Volume I deal with aesthetics; the second three are biographically oriented; and the last two treat themes in individual works.

I am particularly grateful to Dennis Jackson and Lindsey Tucker for their valued help in setting up editorial procedures, corresponding with contributors, and handling major proofreading and editorial work for the journal.

Zack Bowen, General Editor

Irish
Renaissance
Annual I

The *Portrait* as Portrait: Joyce and Impressionism
By Maurice Beebe

Considering how much has been written on James Joyce's *A Portrait of the Artist as a Young Man,* it is surprising that critics have almost entirely overlooked an Italian writer's review of the novel on which Joyce placed his own stamp of approval. He took the trouble to translate a commentary of Diego Angeli and to see that it was published in a 1918 issue of *The Egoist,* the periodical in which the *Portrait* had been serialized. Called in the original "Un Romanzo di Gesuiti," Angeli's critique offers a number of keys to the interpretation of a book that is seen to be both rebellious in its thought and traditional in its use of analytical techniques, which Joyce learned in Jesuit schools. But what strikes me as particularly original in Angeli's description of the *Portrait* is the comparison he draws between Joyce's art and that of the Impressionist painters. "The brushwork of the novel," says Angeli in the English words of Joyce, "reminds one of certain modern paintings in which the planes interpenetrate and the external vision seems to partake of the sensations of the onlooker. . . . The naturalism of Mr. Joyce is impressionist, the profound synthetic naturalism of some pictures of Cézanne or Maquet, the naturalism of the late impressionists."[1]

This affinity with the visual arts is one of the things Joyce probably meant to suggest through his use of the word "portrait" in his title. Because critics have always disagreed on whether Stephen Dedalus is to be taken seriously or viewed ironically, more attention has been devoted to the relative importance of the words "artist" and "young man" in Joyce's title than to the significance of what is after all the key word of that title. Considering what "portrait" implies in terms of the artistic tradition dominant when Joyce began writing may enable me not only to be quite specific about the kind of novel he wanted to write, but also to show how Impressionism profoundly influenced the style and imagery of the novel, the theory of aesthetics expounded by Joyce through Stephen, and certain important aspects of theme and form. Such an approach may even help to resolve the conflict between those who see Stephen as only a "young man" with limited artistic talent and those who feel that he is already a true "artist."

"Portrait" implies a picture, and to a young man of cultivated artistic interests around the turn of the century pictures would imply the several kinds of visual art prevalent then which could be placed under the general heading of Impressionism or Post-Impressionism. Although I cannot trace a direct line of influence from the early Impressionist painters of the 1870s to Joyce's first efforts at fiction, he seems to have been almost as strongly attracted to the visual arts as to music and to have been so knowledgeable about current trends and fashions in painting that he made use of pictorial themes and archetypes in his writing.[2] As for the literary Impressionists, Joyce was well acquainted with the work of Henry James and probably borrowed the title "A Portrait of the Artist" from *The Portrait of a Lady*. We have long known that Joyce admired such Impressionist writers as Gustave Flaubert, George Moore, and Walter Pater; and when he sent the first chapter of the *Portrait* to Ezra Pound, that most perceptive of readers sent it on to *The Egoist* and told Joyce that he could not "usually read prose at all not anybody's in English except James and Hudson and a little Conrad."[3]

Even if Joyce had never heard of Impressionism in art and literature, he would have been affected by the movement. T. S. Eliot said, "Our sensibility is constantly changing as the world about us changes";[4] and the prevailing sensibility when Joyce was growing up and learning the literary craft was shaped by Impressionism. Arnold Hauser calls it "the last universally valid 'European style' and asserts that "the whole philosophy of the last decades of the [nineteenth] century is dependent on it."[5] William Fleming sees Impressionism as a cultural force that united painting, sculpture, architecture, literature, music, and philosophy during the last quarter of that century,[6] and when the first centennial of Impressionist painting was celebrated in a 1974–1975 exhibition, which broke attendance records in both Paris and New York, René Huyghe of the Académie Francaise was able to look back on the phenomenon from a hundred-year perspective that enabled him to see that the Impressionist Era was distinguished by a "collective intellect," which profoundly altered the thinking behind not only the visual arts, literature, and philosophy, but also history and science.[7]

The early Impressionists issued no group manifestoes, and therefore "impressionism" may be defined in many ways. Most explanations of the movement rely, however, on two basic and related assumptions—first, what Monsieur Huyghe calls "the death of matter"; and second, the fusing of subject and object in a way that blends together the one who sees with what he sees. It was fitting, Huyghe says, that "the Impressionists liked to paint the breaking up of ice on rivers and streams," for such scenes reflected a "new understanding of nature . . . : all that connoted the inert and stable was increasingly supplanted by the fluid and impalpable; nature lost its attributes of weight, density, and hardness" until eventually "the Fluid supplanted the Solid."[8] This was true of time as well as space. In the Heraclitan concept of life as flux Arnold Hauser finds the essence of the Impressionist movement: "The dominion of the movement over permanence and continuity, the feeling that every phenomenon is a fleeting and never-to-be-repeated constellation, a wave gliding away on the river of time, the river into which 'one cannot step twice,' is the simplest formula to which impressionism can be reduced."[9]

With the death of matter and the breakdown of a belief in permanence came increasing scepticism about the realness of the world outside the self. Visually everything began to seem misty, contours were blurred, and for the early Impressionist painters "there were no longer any firm, straight lines. Lines floated and moved."[10] As Maria Kronegger puts it, "A world arises in which everything seems to have lost its natural identity. . . . Impressionists are caught up in the transitoriness of all things. The painter Monet, when painting Rouen cathedral, did not directly catch its gothic structure, but an air envelope of a certain density, through which the cathedral could be seen and by which its appearance was modified with every shift of light."[11] In seeking to capture the transitory, evanescent scene before them, the Impressionist painters came to realize that the integrity of their work depended not only on that particular object seen while standing there in that spot at that particular time of day through whatever quality of light the climate of the day and season provided, but also on the person doing the seeing. The true Impressionist, Jules Laforgue insisted, is "a modernist painter endowed with an uncommon sensibility of the eye."[12] When Monet wrote to a friend in 1880 that he was seeking "*instaneity, above all, the envelopment, the same light spread over everywhere,*" he apparently thought that he had to wait for just the right light before continuing work on a painting already started. He could not have known then that there would come a time when, virtually blind, he would have to paint largely from memory. But implicit throughout the Impressionist aesthetic is the assumption that "the act of perception is more important than either the perceived or the perceiver. No longer is there ME . . . on the one hand, and that tree on the other hand; there is only my seeing, retaining, or remembering that tree."[13] In turn the tree becomes a painting of a tree, and if one is truly to comprehend that tree as the artist saw it, he must have powers of vision as intense as those of the artist. Conrad's ringing statement of his mission, "My task . . . is, by the power of the written word to make you hear, to make you feel—it is, before all, to make you *see*,"[14] reminds us that Impressionism implies collaboration between artist and audience. As Albert Guerard puts it, "The . . . central preoccupation of Conrad's technique, the heart of the impressionist aim, is to invite and control the reader's identifications and so subject him to an intense rather than passive experience."[15] The way in which "external vision seems to partake of the sensations of the onlooker" that Diego Angeli had in mind when writing his review of the *Portrait* strikes close to "the heart of the impressionist aim."

One would suppose that Joyce's *Portrait* has been often seen against the rich tradition of the Impressionist era. Such is not the case. Although critics have acknowledged the "impressionistic" qualities of Joyce's style, they have failed to consider the broader implications of his association with the tradition. Even on the matter of style they are rather vague in their understanding of the term. For some an "impressionistic" style seems to imply nothing more than one that is sensuously rich, a mellifluous flow of descriptive images like those to be found in Pater's prose. As early as 1918, however, Scofield Thayer tried to be more specific when he wrote:

> The great Frenchman [Flaubert] did his best to depict things as he saw them, and that is all the word "impressionist," at least in literature, heretofore implied. Joyce has become impressionist in a much more subtle sense. He gives us, especially in *Ulysses,* the streaming impressions, often only subconsciously cognate to one another, of our habitual life—that vague, tepid river of consciousness to which only our ephemeral moments of real will or appetite can give coherence.[16]

And William York Tindall implied a proper understanding of the term when he wrote, "The first three stories of *Dubliners*

and *A Portrait of the Artist* are presented impressionistically
through the consciousness of Stephen, who is made to seem
both subject and object."[17] If it is the fusion of the observer
with what he sees that largely determines an impressionistic
style, then Joyce's frequent use of a Jamesian reflector or
center-of-consciousness would be almost enough in itself to
justify calling him a literary Impressionist. William A. Harms
could have been thinking of Joyce when he offered this
definition: "Literary Impressionism is a style of writing
which gives aesthetic evidence of an author's profound absorption in life as a diaphanous flow of internalized feelings."[18]

Joyce makes use of several stylistic devices associated with
writers of the late nineteenth century who tried to achieve
effects similar to those in Impressionist art. Commenting on
how George Moore's work reflects "the approach of the
impressionist painters wherein vivid details are momentarily
accentuated against a moving blur of undelineated
background," Benjamin Giorgio cites this passage from *A
Mummer's Wife* to illustrate his point: "The two women
looked down into the great pit, through which the crowd was
rolling in one direction, a sort of human tide, a vague tumult
in which little was distinguishable; a bald head or a bunch of
yellow flowers in a woman's bonnet flashed through the
darkness for an instant like the crest of a wave."[19] The use of a
part to suggest the whole may at times result in rather
extravagant use of synecdoche, especially when parts of the
human body are made to act in a peculiarly autonomous way,
as in Moore's " 'What have you got for us?' said four red lips
as Kate entered" or "she made a sign to the ladies, and the
room was left to the flat chests and tweed coats." But the
device can be effective when it is used to suggest a fragmen-
tary or disoriented view of a larger scene. Joyce uses the
device effectively at the beginning of the *Portrait* when
Stephen "was caught in the whirl of a scrimmage and, fearful
of the flashing eyes and muddy boots, bent down to look

through the legs. The fellows were struggling and groaning and their legs were rubbing and kicking and stamping. Then Jack Lawton's yellow boots dodged out the ball and all the other boots and legs ran after."[20]

Joyce's choice of imagery seems strongly influenced by Impressionist practice in his extensive use of water, shadows, clouds, windows, and mirrors. Some art historians date the beginning of Impressionism as a movement from that moment in 1869 when Monet and Renoir met at La Grenouillère and each painted three pictures of the Frog Pond which, though distinguished by individual style, are very much alike in the impression they convey. "Water was the key element to be studied," Howard Greenfeld says of these celebrated paintings, "the movement of water and the varied reflections on water. . . . A study of the play of sunlight in the water, too, gave them deeper insights into the uses of color."[21] According to William Fleming, the early Impressionists liked to paint scenes of water because of "its fluidity, its surface reflections, the perpetual play of changing light"; and with the help of new technical theories about color, they were able "to step up the luminosity of their canvases so as to convey the illusion of sunlight sifted through a prism."[22] It is no accident that the moment of Stephen's consecration as an artist takes place against a setting which Joyce describes as a seascape, but long before then Joyce has made effective use of Impressionist imagery. For instance—

How pale the light was at the window! But that was nice. The fire rose and fell on the wall. It was like waves. Someone had put coal on and he heard voices. They were talking. It was the noise of the waves. Or the waves were talking among themselves as they rose and fell.
He saw the sea of waves, long dark waves rising and falling, dark under the moonless night. A tiny light twinkled at the pierhead where the ship was entering. . . . [26–27]

Irish climate being what it is, there are few sunny scenes in the

Portrait, but Joyce achieves much the same shadowing effect through the use of firelight. At one point "the firelight flickered on the wall and beyond the window a spectral dusk was gathering upon the river" (67–68), and at another

> The chapel was flooded by the dull scarlet light that filtered through the lowered blinds; and through the fissure between the last blind and the sash a shaft of wan light entered like a spear and touched the embossed brasses of the candlesticks upon the altar that gleamed like the battleworn mail armour of angels. [116]

Windows are important in such passages. As Stephen travels with his father by the night train to Cork, he sits in a corner of the railway carriage and gazes out the window:

> He saw the darkening lands slipping past him, the silent tele-graphpoles passing his window swiftly every four seconds, the little glimmering stations, manned by a few silent sentries, flung by the mail behind her and twinkling for a moment in the darkness like fiery grains flung backwards by a runner. [87]

Here Joyce achieves an effect of movement which a painter would have difficulty attaining. It is as if the train were still and what is outside the window were moving ("the silent telegraphpoles passing his window swiftly"), but that feeling gives way to a sensation of rapid movement through time as well as space. Commenting on the "kaleidoscopic effect" of this passage, Maria Kronegger notes that "Joyce creates the impression of blurred images passing before his eyes in total silence by repetition of key words (flung), and by his use of the gerund and adjectival participles. Words take the place of objects: darkening, slipping, passing, glimmering, twinkling, etc."[23] Because the effect of words ending in –ing is to suggest a process of becoming rather than static, fixed being, the reader participates as he himself seems to "travel" through Joyce's narrative.

The Impressionist painters were fond of using pictures within pictures as well as windows and mirrors in order to create an illusion of internal depth. They felt that the use of pictures, mirrors, windows, and doorways served to draw the viewer into the painting by calling attention to the artificial aspects of the larger picture and by subtly reminding the spectator that he is himself taking part in a visual experience. Similarly, it is difficult to read the passage quoted above without being forced to share vicariously Stephen's sensations, for we have all experienced the illusion of both moving and remaining still as we have watched the horizon slip by from a moving vehicle. This is but one of several ways in which Joyce's adaptation of Impressionistic techniques enables him to achieve a sense of identification among artist, character, and reader that helps to justify the world-within-world of his reflexive art.

In addition to being able to depict a progression through space and time, the writer has a further advantage over the painter in that he can make use of other senses than sight. In what amounts to an Impressionistic credo for the literary artist, Conrad insisted that

> the artistic aim when expressing itself in written words must . . . make its appeal through the senses, if its high desire is to reach the secret spring of responsive emotions. It must strenuously aspire to the plasticity of sculpture, to the colour of painting, and to the magic suggestiveness of music—which is the art of arts. And it is only through complete, unswerving devotion to the perfect blending of form and substance; it is only through an unremitting never-discouraged care for the shape and ring of sentences that an approach can be made to plasticity, to colour, and that the light of magic suggestiveness may be brought to play for an evanescent instant over the commonplace surface of words.[24]

How "the shape and ring of sentences" can evoke both the plasticity of visual images and the musical effect of the auditory is well illustrated by this key passage in the *Portrait:*

> He drew forth a phrase from his treasure and spoke it softly to himself:
> —A day of dappled seaborne clouds.
> The phrase and the day and the scene harmonised in a chord. Words. Was it their colours? He allowed them to glow and fade, hue after hue: sunrise gold, the russet and green of apple orchards, azure of waves, the greyfringed fleece of clouds. No, it was not their colours: it was the poise and balance of the period itself. Did he then love the rhythmic rise and fall of words better than their associations of legend and colour? Or was it that, being as weak of sight as he was shy of mind, he drew less pleasure from the reflection of the glowing sensible world through the prism of a language manycoloured and richly storied than from the contemplation of an inner world of individual emotions mirrored perfectly in a lucid supple periodic prose? [166–67]

Here auditory effects blend with the visual imagery. Throughout his reveries Stephen moves easily from one sense to others. Thus the sound of the word "suck" evokes the visual image of water draining from the wash basin of a lavatory in the Wicklow Hotel, and when he remembered "the white look of the lavatory" and the faucets marked hot and cold, "he felt cold and then a little hot" (11). And if words have colors, sounds may have feelings: "There were different kinds of pains for all the different kinds of sounds. A long thin cane would have a high whistling sound and he wondered what was that pain like. It made him shivery to think of it and cold" (45). If the reader too feels a tremor as he reads the sentence, then Joyce has tapped what Conrad calls "the secret spring of responsive emotions" and thus achieved one of the aims of Impressionist prose.

Several aspects of the aesthetic theory presented in *Stephen Hero* and the *Portrait* seem to be closely related to Impressionism. Stephen's explanation of the three essential qualities of beauty—wholeness, harmony, and radiance—is particularly significant in this regard. By showing that these three qualities correspond to three stages of aesthetic apprehension, Joyce equates the objective beauty of the art work with the subjective process by which it is seen, thus insisting that a collaboration between the artist and his viewer is necessary to art. As Stephen expounds his theory to his friend Lynch in the *Portrait,* he uses a basket as his example of an object to be perceived, but when he says that "the first phase of apprehension is a bounding line drawn about the object to be apprehended," it is as if he were describing a framed picture:

> . . . the esthetic image is first luminously apprehended as self-bounded and selfcontained upon the immeasurable background of space or time which is not it. You apprehend it as *one* thing. You see it as one whole. You apprehend its wholeness. That is *integritas*. [212]

Stephen moves on easily to the second quality:

> —Then, said Stephen, you pass from point to point, led by its formal lines; you apprehend it as balanced part against part within its limits; you feel the rhythm of its structure. In other words the synthesis of immediate perception is followed by the analysis of apprehension. Having first felt that it is *one* thing you feel now that it is a *thing.* You apprehend it as complex, multiple, divisible, separable, made up of its parts, the result of its parts and their sum, harmonious. That is *consonantia*. [212]

But he hesitates over the third term he has borrowed from Aquinas. In *Stephen Hero* Joyce acknowledged a religious dimension to art when he had Stephen define *claritas* in terms of "epiphany," equating the radiance of the art object with its "soul" and using other religious imagery in defining the final stage of apprehension of that "moment" which is the art-work: "Its soul, its whatness, leaps to us from the vestment of its appearance. The soul of the commonest object . . . seems to us radiant. The object achieves its epiphany."[25] In the *Portrait* version, however, words like "epiphany," "soul,"

and "vestments" are avoided as Stephen offers an entirely
secular definition of *claritas*. He tells Lynch that he has
rejected Aquinas's notion that

> *claritas* is the artistic discovery and representation of the divine
> purpose in anything or a force of generalisation which would
> make the esthetic image a universal one, make it outshine its
> proper conditions. But that is literary talk. I understand it so.
> When you have apprehended that basket as one thing and have
> then analysed it according to its form and apprehended it as a
> thing you make the only synthesis which is logically and estheti-
> cally permissable. You see that it is that thing which it is and no
> other thing. The radiance of which he speaks is the scholastic
> *quidditas*, the *whatness* of a thing. [213]

Hence, in keeping with Joyce's initial insistence that art is a
form of stasis rather than a kinetic force propelling the
observer to something beyond the art work itself, Joyce now
rejects all implications of symbolism or idealism as he equates
the radiance of the work of art with its simple, objective
whatness.

Although Joyce himself rejected the idea of epiphany, it
remains a valid concept in literary criticism. It is a convenient
term to apply to those moments of sudden insight which
mark, for instance, the climaxes of the stories in *Dubliners*.
Judging, however, from the modest collection of *Epiphanies*
which Joyce himself wrote, he was less likely to find
epiphanies in dramatic or significant actions than in those
"minor, unimpressive, random events" which Erich Auer-
bach considers one of the hallmarks of modern literature.[26]
Joyce's epiphanies are closely related to the images of Pound's
Imagism, the "air-blown grains" of Henry James, the "es-
sences" of Marcel Proust, and Virginia Woolf's "moments of
being." But it does not seem to be widely recognized that an
emphasis on separate moments of perception in twentieth-
century literature may owe much to the revolution in the
visual arts which occurred during the era of Impressionism.

From the constantly changing flux of life, the Impressionist painters attempted to capture in that flash perception they called *vistazo* an isolated snapshot of reality. Painters have always had to deal with single instants, but whereas earlier artists preferred to depict moments of intense dramatic action or to freeze life in a way that would suggest significance beyond the object represented, it was "only the Impressionists," John Rewald tells us, who "pursued the instant for the instant's sake, not as the climax of biblical or historical or mythological events, not as a symbol, not as a distillation of intimate visions, but as the immediate response of their retinas and brushes to their observations of nature."[27]

The reluctance of the Impressionists to depict significant scenes, preferring instead what often seemed to be only random or trivial, is one reason why initial public and critical response to their work was hostile. Similarly when Stephen Dedalus of *Stephen Hero* offered some of his ideas about aesthetics before the Literary and Historical Society of University College, his listeners were unsympathetic because his insistence on the formal autonomy of art would absolve the artist from moral and patriotic obligations. That separation is, of course, one of the main points of Stephen's aesthetic. Joyce knew that in the realm of ethics art is not to be confused with artist, but as far as art itself is concerned, he did indeed insist that what matters is the simple, static presence of the art work rather than any abstract meaning or lesson that might be found in it. The Impressionist painters annoyed philistine visitors to their exhibitions by demanding that their paintings be viewed not as windows on the world, but simply as paintings. Clement Greenberg makes a significant statement about this aspect of their work:

> Realistic, illusionist art had dissembled the medium, using art to conceal art. Modernism used art to call attention to art. The limitations that constitute the medium of painting—the flat surface, the shape of the support, the properties of pigment—were

treated by the Old Masters as negative factors that could be acknowledged only implicitly or indirectly. Modernist painting has come to regard these same limitations as positive factors that are to be acknowledged openly. Manet's paintings became the first Modernist ones by virtue of the frankness with which they declared the surfaces on which they were painted. The Impressionists, in Manet's wake, abjured underpainting and glazing, to leave the eye under no doubt as to the fact that the colors used were made of real paint that came from pots or tubes. Cézanne sacrificed verisimilitude, or correctness, in order to fit drawing and design more explicitly to the rectangular shape of the canvas.[28]

It is not far from the Impressionist painters to those writers who insist on calling attention to the media and materials with which they work. In *The Pound Era* Hugh Kenner says that a distinguishing feature of Modernist literature is its insistence on "space-craft." We may think of Henry James's *The Ambassadors,* for example, as a narrative occupying a period of time, but the book itself "is a hundred cubic inches of wood pulp."[29] Henry James would not have put it so bluntly, but the first of the major Impressionist writers certainly saw his novels as physical blocks of matter which were to be divided into units called paragraphs and chapters.

Applying Joyce's notion of *claritas* to the *Portrait* and thereby emphasizing the *whatness* of the work helps to justify certain aspects of the novel's form. In spite of the fact that the narrative proceeds chronologically from Stephen's infancy to early manhood, the *Portrait* is a much more static work than its predecessor. Whereas *Stephen Hero* was written mostly in conventional summary narrative, the *Portrait* is developed largely by means of distinct scenes. This is widely recognized, of course, but we can better understand why the novel is written scenically if we place it against the context of the Impressionist era and realize that in fiction Impressionism was found not only in works by James, Conrad, and other writers who used a center-of-consciousness technique or filtered everything seen through a detached narrator, but also in the *vistazo*-like slices of life depicted by Chekhov, Katherine Mansfield, and, of course, the Joyce of *Dubliners*. If we say that the contents of that collection seem more like "sketches" than stories, it is partly because there is an obvious analogy between those works and the visual arts.

The *whatness* of the *Portrait* begins literally with the words "A Portrait" in its title. The story begins in a ragged, rough-edged way with Stephen in infancy, his mind a confused jumble of baby-talk, but little by little as the novel progresses he emerges as a clearly distinct character until finally his essential nature is, as it were, distilled. In an important article on "The Imaginary Portrait: Fin-de-siècle Icon," Jan B. Gordon has shown how "at the conclusion of *A Portrait* there is no longer the voice of a character but of a Stephen who, as surely as Dorian Gray, victimized by another Portrait, has refined himself out of human existence. He literally *is* his art."[30] We are given a set-piece demonstration of Stephen the artist by means of the villanelle he composes, a romantic lyric which bids farewell to romantic yearning, and finally at the end of the work there are extracts from Stephen's diary. Why Joyce's *Portrait* ends in this way has never been fully explained, but the device may be understood in part as a heritage from the Impressionist tradition. Commenting on the use of diaries in fiction by the French Impressionist writers, Maria Kronegger points out that "writers of diaries, notebooks, and memoirs have the advantage of making everything proceed from a certain instant: according to the moment, they can change writing styles, that is the manner of suggesting reality; they can change points of view in order to capture the most volatile moments of life together with nuances of color and tone, and to seize in passing the variations in aspect which the same scene assumes at different moments."[31] In other words, short diary entries can be seen as verbal equivalents to the *vistazos* recorded visually by

Impressionist painters. Appropriately therefore one of
Stephen's diary entries is almost like a little Frog Pond
painting. We have seen that earlier in the novel Stephen
speculated on the implications of the phrase "a day of dappled
seaborne clouds" as something of a touchstone for the kind of
art he wanted to create. Now he again combines images of
clouds, waves, and even an apple orchard, but in a much more
concise way which seems to offer his own objective demonstration that he has become an artist committed to life as seen:

> *5 April:* Wild spring. Scudding clouds. O life! Dark stream of
> swirling bogwater on which appletrees have cast down their
> delicate flowers. Eyes of girls among the leaves. Girls demure and
> romping. All fair or auburn: no dark ones. They blush better.
> Houp-la! [250]

That little set-piece may or may not be a convincing
example of Stephen as artist, but if I have presented enough
evidence thus far to support the claim that the novel could
have been titled "A Portrait of the Impressionist Artist as a
Young Man," some of the problems readers have encountered
in dealing with Stephen may be explained away. It seems to
me obvious enough that Joyce intended us to see a progression towards some kind of artistic maturity in Stephen. That
progression is represented through certain key episodes
which revolve around the theme of vision, beginning with the
traumatic episode of Stephen's broken glasses and proceeding
through such phases as his deliberate attempt "to mortify the
sense of sight" by making it "his rule to walk in the street
with downcast eyes" (150) until finally during his moment of
consecration as artist he proceeds from a sense that "darkness
was falling" over the scene before him until he realizes that "it
was not darkness that fell from the air. It was brightness"
(232–34). Recognizing this progression from varying degrees
and kinds of blindness to seeing things not necessarily clearly
but brightly should help us to realize also the way in which

Impressionism influenced the point-of-view used in the novel. Just as the Impressionist painters insisted that it was their superior vision rather than just the objects they depicted which justified their work, Joyce located *claritas* not only in the whatness of the work of art but in the eye of the beholder. We have seen that throughout his exposition of the three qualities of beauty Stephen equates *integritas, consonantia,* and *claritas* with the three stages of aesthetic apprehension. In *Stephen Hero* he was even more specific than in the *Portrait,* in the earlier work using not a basket but the clock of the Ballast Office as his example of an aesthetic object:

> —Imagine my glimpses at that clock as the gropings of a spiritual eye which seeks to adjust its vision to an exact focus. The moment the focus is reached the object is epiphanised. It is just in this epiphany that I find the third, the supreme quality of beauty.[32]

Stephen does not achieve that kind of focus until near the end of the novel in which he appears. Until then the method carefully used by Joyce enables him to depict not so much his mature view of his younger self as Stephen's own view of himself and the world around him. The often maligned style of the *Portrait* may thus be defended as Joyce's quite brilliant effort to show how life might have been viewed by an archetypal young artist at the turn of the century who had not yet found his own separate and unique identity.[33] If that artist was, as I have tried to show, an Impressionist, it was to be expected that what he viewed might often appear to be shimmery, diaphanous, and evanescent.

NOTES

1. Reprinted in *James Joyce: The Critical Heritage,* ed. Robert H. Deming, 2 vols. (New York: Barnes and Noble, 1970), 1:115–16. Angeli's critique was first published in *Il Marzocco* (Florence) 22 (12 August 1917): 2–3.

2. See, for example, Archie K. Loss, "The Pre-Raphaelite Woman, the Symbolist *Femme-Enfant*, and the Girl with Long Flowing Hair in the Earlier Work of Joyce," *Journal of Modern Literature* 3 (February 1973): 3–23.

3. Ezra Pound to James Joyce, January 1914, in *Pound/Joyce: The Letters of Ezra Pound to James Joyce, with Pound's Essays on Joyce* (New York: New Directions, 1966), p. 24.

4. T. S. Eliot, "The Social Function of Poetry," in *On Poetry and Poets* (New York: Farrar, Straus and Cudahy, 1957), p. 10.

5. Arnold Hauser, *The Social History of Art,* 2 vols. (New York: Knopf, 1951), 2: 869–926.

6. William Fleming, *Arts and Ideas,* 3rd ed. (New York: Holt, Rinehart and Winston, 1968), pp. 477–500.

7. René Huyghe, "Shifts in Thought During the Impressionist Era: Painting, Science, Literature, History, and Philosophy," in *Impressionism: A Centenary Exhibition* (New York: Metropolitan Museum of Art, 1974–75), pp. 14–32.

8. Huyghe, pp. 18–21.

9. Hauser, *Social History,* 2: 872.

10. Huyghe, "Shifts in Thought," p. 22.

11. Maria Elisabeth Kronegger, *Literary Impressionism* (New Haven, Conn.: College and University Press, 1973), pp. 45–46.

12. "Impressionism," in Linda Nochlin, ed., *Impressionism and Post-Impressionism, 1874–1904: Sources and Documents* (Englewood Cliffs, N.J.: Prentice-Hall, 1966), p. 15.

13. Kronegger, *Literary Impressionism,* p. 40.

14. Joseph Conrad, "Preface" to *The Nigger of the "Narcissus."*

15. Albert J. Guerard, *Conrad the Novelist* (Cambridge, Mass.: Harvard University Press, 1958), p. 152.

16. "James Joyce," *Dial* 65 (19 September 1918): 201–03.

17. William York Tindall, *James Joyce: His Way of Interpreting the Modern World* (London: Scribner's, 1950), p. 40.

18. William A. Harms, "Impressionism as a Literary Style" (Ph.D. diss., Indiana University, 1971), p. 35.

19. Benjamin David Giorgio, "Stephen Crane: American Impressionist" (Ph. D. diss., University of Wisconsin, 1969), p. 17ff.

20. *A Portrait of the Artist as a Young Man* (New York: Viking Press, 1965), pp. 9–10. Subsequent references are included parenthetically in the text.

21. Howard Greenfeld, *The Impressionist Revolution* (Garden City, N. Y.: Doubleday, 1972), p. 67.

22. Fleming, *Arts,* pp. 485, 483.

23. Kronegger, *Literary Impressionism,* p. 78.

24. Conrad in "Preface" to *The Nigger of the "Narcissus".*

25. James Joyce, *Stephen Hero,* ed. Theodore Spencer (New York: New Directions, 1955), p. 213.

26. As cited by Morris Beja, *Epiphany in the Modern Novel* (Seattle, Wash.: University of Washington Press, 1971), p. 17.

27. John Rewald, *The Impressionist Brush* (New York: Metropolitan Museum of Art, 1974), p. 54.

28. Clement Greenberg, "Modernist Painting," in Gregory Battcock, ed. *The New Art: A Critical Anthology,* new rev. ed. (New York: E. P. Dutton, 1973), pp. 68–69.

29. Hugh Kenner, *The Pound Era* (Berkeley and Los Angeles: University of California Press, 1971), p. 28.

30. Jan B. Gordon, "The Imaginary Portrait: Fin-de-siècle Icon," *University of Windsor Review* 5 (Fall 1969): 99-100.

31. Kronegger, *Literary Impressionism*, p. 51.

32. Joyce, *Stephen Hero*, p. 211.

33. This view of the novel is argued persuasively by James Naremore in "Style as Meaning in *A Portrait of the Artist*," *James Joyce Quarterly* 4 (Summer 1967): 331–42.

'Tis Mysterious Surely and Fantastic Strange: Art and Artists in Three Plays of George Fitzmaurice

By John Cooke

In George Fitzmaurice's *The Magic Glasses*, Jaymony Shanahan perches in the loft of his family cottage, and with his set of glasses envisions "the seven wonders of the world, seas and mountains and cities," and conjures passionate love affairs with "the purtiest women was ever seen on the globe." But he can be "cured" of his hallucinations if he will daily "hop on one leg and make a bow East and West and North and South" and "turn the red earth" from sunup to sundown.

The Pie-Dish centers upon old Leum Donoghue, who has spent twenty years making a pie-dish "and thirty years before that thinking of it." Leum's grandson Eugene knows "it's great wonders are in that pie-dish," adorned by Leum's hand with "putty figarios."

Roger Carmody, the maker of "dandy dolls" in Fitzmaurice's play of the same name, no sooner completes a masterpiece than the Hag's Son, the "Barna brat," will "come at it, give it a knuckle in the navel, split it in two fair halves, collar the windpipe, and off with him carrying the squeaky-squeak," leaving "Roger raging." As a consequence, his compulsion to steal Father James's geese overwhelms him. Eating three geese at a sitting, Roger turns into "a mangy vomiting snooker" wearing "a damn ugly smile."

Are Fitzmaurice's plays, like Roger, "teetotally mad it-self"? Certainly. Incomprehensible? Maybe not.

The Pie-Dish (1907), *The Dandy Dolls* (1908), and *The Magic Glasses* (c.1908) are indeed disturbing in their extravagant eccentricity, so disturbing that producers have been reluctant to tackle them, and serious and thorough criticism is rare. And no wonder. The ebullient comic language and frenetic tone of these intense one-acters seduce both audience and critic. Because Fitzmaurice's subject is the very elusiveness of imagination and belief, the reader in search of "meaning" finds himself inside a world in which such moonstruck dialogue and manic business lead straight into subjectivity and solipsism. Sometimes Fitzmaurice's sing–song yellow brick roads go nowhere.

The escape from this enigma depends at least in part on placing this playwright within a context. George Fitzmaurice (1877–1963) gained his artistic identity as a popular Abbey dramatist, contemporary with Yeats, Synge, and Colum. But these playwrights share more than the coincidence of talent and nationality: many of their plays reflect a concern for art and the artist in Irish society. Inevitably their themes encompass a treatment of the role of the artist, the function of art, and the nature of the artists' audience. To readers of Colum's *The Fiddler's House,* Synge's *The Playboy of the Western World,* and Yeats's *The King's Threshold,* this information is of course not new. But interpreters of Fitzmaurice, though they often tag Roger, Leum, and Jaymony as artists, fail to employ this conventional theme to illuminate his plays satisfactorily. This theme, I think, may allow us to enjoy the seductive flamboyance of these plays and appreciate Fitzmaurice's compelling treatment of a major theme in modern Irish drama.

The significance of this theme will emerge only from an initial understanding of the traditional image of the Irish poet-artist, long a central concern of the modern Irish writer. If the Irish Literary Renaissance wished to see anything

reborn, it was the power of native art and the social stability
of the native artist. For too many centuries the Congreves,
Swifts, Wildes, and Shaws played parts—prominent parts—in
England's literary history, not Ireland's. Seeking to reverse
this situation, Yeats often refers to the traditional status of the
ancient Irish artist as both a model and a goal for contemporary writers.

Reference to the power and status of the Celtic artist
saturates early Irish history. The highest–ranked poets com-
manded the same honor price as the tribal kings, and enjoyed
equal status with them; according to tradition, both derived
their peculiar power from the pagan gods.[1] Because of the
immense power of his art, the poet maintained high official
status in the court.[2] His art, in service of the king, could
insure bountiful harvests or plentiful and beautiful children,
good health, or great fortune in love and war. Not surpris-
ingly, an art which provided joy and plenty could also
conjure fear and destruction. The poet's satires were magical.
He traditionally made excessive demands on the king; "no
one dared refuse [poets] anything because of the harm they
could do with their satires."[3]

The artist's power for both good and evil insured him a
special relation to the king and, hence, to the community.
Though his function was communal and public, his art remained unsullied by compromise. The poet was not simply
the court's over-talented, versifying lapdog; his art de-
manded, and received, independence.[4]

When the tribal kingdoms dissolved in the seventeenth
century—and along with them the poet's official sanction—
the artist's independence and supernatural powers remained
linked, consciously or subconsciously, with paganism.
Hence, orthodox Catholic Ireland viewed the artist with
suspicion. Though he remained a prominent feature of Irish
society, he stood outside its mainstream. This separation of
the poet/artist from society lies at the core of the plays which
I discuss hereafter.

Yeats's *The King's Threshold* centers on the poet Seanchan, who is fasting because the king has denied him the "old right of the poets"[5] to sit at councils of state. Yeats's poet retains many of the powers of the ancient poet, though his characterization reflects Yeats's exceedingly romantic interpretation of the Irish bard. Seanchan demands independence for both himself and his art, and is conscious of his effect on beauty and procreation. Alternately cajoling and threatening Seanchan, the King attempts to restore order and free himself from the poet's challenge. Ignoring each offer, Seanchan finally dies.

Synge's Christy Mahon and Colum's Conn Hourican are artists as well, but these countrymen lack the conscious, studied self-image of Yeats's Seanchan. Both *Playboy* and *The Fiddler's House* portray the hero's developing awareness of himself as an artist. Christy enters the pub a "soft lad" and a "little smiling fellow." No one takes him seriously—not even himself—until he spins his tale of killing his "da." Suddenly, his self-image alters:

> Pegeen: Wasn't I telling you, and you a fine, handsome young
> fellow with a noble brow.
> Christy: Is it me?[6]

He admits his own wonder at the change: "Up to the day I killed my father, there wasn't a person in Ireland knew the kind I was, and I there drinking, waking, eating, sleeping, a quiet, simple poor fellow with no man giving me heed" (*PWW* 29). Suddenly, the countryfolk liken Christy's "savagery" and "fine words" (*PWW* 67) to those of the poet: "I've heard all times it's the poets are your like—fine, fiery fellows with great rages when their temper's roused" (*PWW* 28). Ultimately, Christy becomes the savage poet of their (and his own) imagination. Christy's audience, gradually learning to differentiate "between a gallous story and a dirty deed" (*PWW* 74) may cool in their affection for him, but the hero

himself continues to answer his own question—"Is it
me?"—with firmer and bolder visions of his deed until at last
he shuns his bewildered opponents to "go romancing through
a romping lifetime from this hour to the dawning of the
judgment day" (*PWW* 77).

Like Christy, the hero of *The Fiddler's House* also affirms
his role as artist. Conn Hourican, a renowned fiddler who has
left the world of fairs and pubs and endless wandering to
settle on his small farm with his daughters, soon realizes the
land stifles his creativity. "Since you settled down," he is
told, "you lost your art."[7] Like Seanchan and the ancient
bards, Conn's art demands freedom. "The man of art must
have his listeners" (*FH* 13) who will give him "his due after
all, honour and respect" (*FH* 20). Realizing this, Conn turns
over his land to his acquisitive but industrious son–in–law,
James Moynihan, and takes to the road to regain his status,
and, it is suggested, reconfirm the power of all Irish artists.
James toasts Conn before he departs: "Here's to the
fiddler. . . . May it be again like in the days of Ireland's
glory, when the men of art had their rights and their dues"
(*FH* 60).

In *The Pie-Dish, The Magic Glasses,* and *The Dandy Dolls,*
Fitzmaurice, too, deals with the dissolution of the traditional
relationship between artist and society, although, as the plots
reveal, such a generalization cannot account for his bizarre
treatment and presentation of this conventional theme.

The Pie-Dish, a thin play and Fitzmaurice's least interesting
dramatically, premiered at the Abbey only a year after the
riotous opening of Synge's *Playboy.* In it, as stated previously, old Leum Donoghue has dedicated fifty years to
making a pie-dish—thirty to its planning, the last twenty in
its execution.[8] The dish nears completion, requiring only a
few more "putty figarios," but Leum is dying fast, and his
daughters wish Father Troy to administer last rites immediately. Clutching the dish to his chest, Leum refuses the
sacrament. "It's time I must get—if it isn't time from God I'll

get, maybe the devil will give me time."[9] Both deny his request. Leum shakes, the dish falls from his hands and shatters, and he dies.

Roger Carmody, an eccentric but renowned maker of "dandy dolls," shares Leum's obsession with his craft, having been "forty years at dolls."[10] The Grey Man, an Otherworldly figure from the "Isle of Doon," arrives at Roger's cottage to purchase his handiwork. But the Grey Man must contend with a rival, the son of the Hag of Barna, who has broken every previous doll and is expected to attack again that evening. Meanwhile, Father James, an ally of Roger's wife, Cauth, adds a third faction. Every time Roger's dolls are snatched, his addiction for "going marauding after poultry in the dark" overtakes him. Sadly, the poultry is most often Father James's, who therefore maintains an interest in defending the doll from the Hag's Son. When the latter arrives, a violent skirmish ensues which terminates, once the Hag's Son succeeds in smashing the doll, with an explosion. When order is restored, we hear of Roger "being carried away by the Hag and the Son of the Hag. . . . Galloping like the wind they were, through the pass of the Barna mountains, sweeping him along with them, for ever and ever, to their woeful den in the heart of the Barna hills" (DD 37).

Jaymony Shanahan—the visionary poet and musician of *The Magic Glasses*—is no better off. With "magic glasses" purchased from a "brown woman," Jaymony can not only make eerie music, but can envision palaces, armies, and beautiful women, which offer him "the pleasure and diversion of the world" (MG 12). Convinced he is sick, his parents send for Morgan Quille, a folk doctor, who "cures" him momentarily. Jaymony's enthusiasm for normalcy quickly wanes, however, and as his parents rejoice at his cure, Jaymony slips back into the loft and commences a frantic dance. As the loft crashes to the floor, the broken glasses slash Jaymony's jugular and he dies.

Fitzmaurice's artworks and artists hardly resemble those

found in Yeats, Synge, and Colum, nor is the relation between art, artist, and the onstage audience simple and direct.
A comparison remains profitable, however. By locating and
describing the differences in their treatment of art, artist and
audience, and the factors which contribute to these differences, we may find Fitzmaurice's incongruities less incongru-
ous. Further, we may correct some of the critical misin-
terpretations to which Fitzmaurice's plays have been sub-
jected. This comparison will begin with an examination of
how this playwright treats each of the three major factors—
the artist, the artwork, and the community—in terms of the
aesthetic and symbolic qualities of the artwork and the self-
image, role, and function of both artist and audience.

Jaymony, Leum, and Roger, unlike Christy, Conn, and
Seanchan, do not see themselves as artists. They recognize no
audience, nor do they possess any sense of their function
within the community. In his introduction to Fitzmaurice's
Dramatic Fantasies, Austin Clarke refers to Jaymony as a
"natural,"[11] and this seems an accurate description of these
elusive characters. "Natural" here is not intended to mean, as
one definition has it, "a half-wit, naturally deficient in intellect." Fitzmaurice's artists are crazy, but not stupid. Rather,
by calling them "naturals," I wish to emphasize their complete lack of self–consciousness, their freedom from con-
straint, artificiality, and affectation. This is not to say they are
paragons of deportment; hardly so—their freedom from con-
straint often includes freedom from propriety, grace, manners, and common sense.

Having little concept of community, Fitzmaurice's naturals
ignore its values and beliefs, especially those which emphasize
obligations to a day's labor, to family, marriage, and the
Catholic Church. Cauth complains that Roger should "exert
himself in a proper labouring man, earn his coin for himself"
(*DD* 22). Leum's daughter Johanna grumbles that "before we
heard talks of a pie-dish come from him," he was "always an
industrious man about the fields" (*P-D* 54). When Morgan

Quille interrogates Jaymony prior to the "cure," his first question is "Are you Catholic?" (*MG* 10). Part of Quille's cure requires that Jaymony labor—"turn the red earth"—from sunup to sundown. Further, none of Fitzmaurice's heroes seems interested in family. Jaymony sees women only in his visions; Leum makes no mention of his wife and hates his children; and, in the most intriguing example, Roger's child is but an "ashy creature . . . with the map of the world painted on his burnt spangled shins" (*DD* 21), an ironic contrast to the perfection he demands of his artificial off-spring, his "dandy dolls."

The natural does not discount the obligations of family and church because his beliefs differ, but because such concerns lie outside his realm of being. Fitzmaurice does not endow his artists with values; separate from the artwork, they are almost devoid of identity. We gain what little we know through their reaction to others. Jaymony's mother, Maineen, calls one of Jaymony's policeman brothers "a great man for law and order," but for Jaymony both brothers are but "ignorant peelers" (*MG* 11). This visionary prefers his glasses to "being in the slush—same old thing every day—this an ugly spot, and the people ignorant, grumpy, and savage" (*MG* 11).[12] But through such exchanges and antagonisms we simply learn what the artist is not; we remain largely ignorant of him separate from his long-lived, enigmatic obsession with a bizarre work of art. Fitzmaurice's artists, like Blake, seem to have created a system of their own, but this system—if we can call it that—exceeds our comprehension.

Fitzmaurice's artists and the community actually exist in two different worlds. The artwork forces their undesired and ill-fated conjunction. Because the artist's identity is insepara-ble from his art, and because the community's values and beliefs emerge largely in response to this peculiar art/artist relationship, the artwork itself stands at the center of Fitzmaurice's plays and controls our understanding of them.

Art in Fitzmaurice is not only different in kind from that

found in Synge, Yeats, and Colum, but it also performs a different function. As art, fiddle music exists independent of Conn Hourican, just as poetry has significance separate from Seanchan and Christy. The aesthetic value of art remains unquestioned. Therefore, the relation between art and artist, and art and audience, is simple and direct. In *Playboy*, for example, a logical relationship exists between Christy, his "fine words" and "poetry talk," and the inspired devotion with which the folk of Mayo embrace him. Conversely, the artwork in Fitzmaurice's plays has no public, objective value. Instead of encountering Conn's fiddle music or the extravagant words of Christy and Seanchan, the "art" one discovers here is a pie-dish, or a home-made doll, or "magic glasses." Each possesses no value or meaning outside the playworld itself. And whereas Christy grows to understand the power of his art, Fitzmaurice's central characters do not.

Considering the artwork's triviality and insignificance, critics usually find it an amusing oddity or lose sight of the text altogether and assume meaning which simply is not there.[13] When, for example, J. D. Riley refers to the pie-dish's "abstract beauty," one craves (but is denied) further elucidation; for if the dish were beautiful, we would have a new play on our hands, one in which Leum's daughters would be bad critics of abstract art rather than reactionary and suspicious countryfolk, and Leum would no longer be the eccentric peasant looney but an early Magritte or Dali. Clearly, our understanding of these plays depends upon taking Hamlet's advice and speaking no more than is set down for us.

The plays themselves reveal very little about the artwork. Leum simply intends to show his pie-dish, once completed, to his old friends Black Jack of Scartaglen, Moll of Carraweira, and Teigue of Glounaneinta. Roger's dolls—though an inordinately prized commodity in the Otherworld—are innocuous in themselves and provide Roger with nothing more than a prodigious appetite.

The magic glasses offer a more touchy problem since we

know that for *some* reason Padden and Aunts Mary and Jug become stuck to the ladder as they attempt to drag Jaymony from the loft. Since no other evidence attributes this power to the devil, the magic, then, is Jaymony's alone, and he gains his power, one assumes, from the glasses. But importantly, Jaymony never displays his powers until the end of the play; his magic never actually affects the development of the action. Throughout the play, his glasses, like the dolls and the pie-dish, remain in themselves without objective significance.

Because the artworks attain no objective utility or aesthetic value, their primary function emerges from their symbolic rather than aesthetic properties. It would be marvelously convenient to be able to pinpoint exactly what these objects symbolize, but these plays prohibit such precision. The objects as symbols do not function in that manner. Instead, they are voids into which both the community and the artist project meaning. The act of labeling this void—thus making it comprehensible—constitutes the essential action of each play.

When, at the conclusion of *The Dandy Dolls*, Father James sums up the action with " 'Tis mysterious surely, and fantastic strange" (*DD* 37), he typifies the community's response toward both artwork and artist. The words "mystery" and "mysterious" recur often in reference to both. In *The Magic Glasses*, Jaymony's mother Maineen accuses Padden, her husband, of being "too shy . . . to seek out the hidden mystery" (*MG* 9). On first seeing Leum's handiwork, Father Troy exclaims, "A pie-dish! What mysteries are here?" (*P-D* 53). The community is never long content with such elusive, unnamable strangeness. They counter this mysterious presence with explanations adequate to their own highly structured, culture-bound world view. In *The Pie-Dish*, an exchange between Leum's grandsons, Jack and Eugene, illustrates this process:

> Jack: Eugene, it's an ignorant workingman I am, as you know, but it's a great scholard you are, and if there's

> brain-work in that pie-dish it isn't dull of it you can
> be. . . . It's pinching me in to find out what ingenuity
> is in it, Eugene. . . .
>
> Eugene: Jack, I don't know no more than the dead, but all the
> same, as sure as I am telling it to you, it's great wonders
> are in that pie-dish. [*P-D* 45]

But Jack's curiosity soon turns to malice. Instead of simply an
odd ornament, "It's foolery it is" (*P-D* 45). Soon the community projects moral values onto the object; it becomes, for
no logical reason, an "old *pagan* pie-dish" (*P-D* 50, italics
mine). In *The Magic Glasses*, Padden attempts to explain the
"strange music" by a common folk legend: "is it a fairy, then,
that's in the top loft and our Jaymony swept away?" In
following Quille's suggestion that Jaymony's "queer music"
is "entirely like what they do be playing in Teernanogue,"
Padden too associates art and artist with the pagan Other-
world.

The community sees such paganism as a moral threat.
Quille likens Jaymony's account of his visions to those of the
bardic poets:

> Quille: The inspiration is coming on me, for I knew a sort of a
> poet—"out of the mists they come," said he, "one by
> one—out of the mists and the fantastic quagmires of the
> South, their sabres gleaming in the light of the moon."
> Isn't it them you see?
>
> Jaymony: The same. [*MG* 13]

But for Maineen, this mysticism is "immoral talk," and
Padden confirms that it has been "two months now since he
was at church or chapel, and 'tis years since he seen a priest"
(*MG* 12). Soon it is the devil himself behind this strangeness.
Roger's dolls are more than just "trumpery" (*DD* 24); there's
"devilment of course in them dandy dolls" (*DD* 31), just as
Margaret claims, "It's devilment must be in that pie-dish"
(*P-D* 54). Such antics leave "a bad name on [Roger's] house"
(*DD* 31).

Whatever evil paganism and devilment the community projects onto the artworks quite naturally pertains to the creators as well. Not only is Roger a "looney fool," but when obsessed, Cauth claims, he wears "no sort of expression . . . ever seen on the face of a Christian" (*DD* 24). Indeed, later she imagines in his face "the countenance of the devil" (*DD* 27). A passage late in *The Pie-Dish* illustrates how Father Troy, after questioning the "mysteries" in Leum's creation, answers himself through progressive condemnations of the artist. First he suspects "lunacy." When Margaret discounts this theory, Troy assumes "It's wicked he is, then." This wickedness takes a more tangible direction in Troy's final assertions: "It's the devil himself has Leum Donoghue body and soul" (*P-D* 54). The same pattern applies even more forcefully in *The Magic Glasses*. When other explanations for Jaymony's "sickness" prove insufficient, Jaymony becomes a "haunted thing" (*MG* 10). The fantastic conclusion reveals the extent to which the community demands comprehensible labels for what they experience. When Padden, Mary, and Jug stick to the ladder, " 'Tis the devil has us fast," not just Jaymony's power. Of course, Jaymony, lying dead in the rubble, sports neither cloven hooves nor horns. In their imagination, Jaymony has progressed from mere sickness to lunacy to demonic possession itself. As in the other plays, the community here attempts to contain the strangeness of art and artist within its conventional sphere of understanding. The people can accept Jaymony as sick or even possessed by the devil, but he cannot be the strange artist/visionary unaccountable to the community. One must recall Jaymony's "cure": after he turns the red earth,

> . . . in the dusk he'll ramble to the neighbours' houses and discourse on cattle and on crops and all things on the agricultural way. He'll go to market and to fair—take drink—a little—and ketch a woman if he wants to when he is coming home. On the twenty-first day a farmer's daughter is to be made out for Jaymony Shanahan. [*MG* 13]

Jaymony will then epitomize conventional Irish manhood.

Why does the community attack Fitzmaurice's artists? Why do they need to call Jaymony's "pleasure and diversion of the world" a symptom of sickness and even possession? Superficially, the community cannot endure the public ridicule their association with the artist engenders. Jaymony's brothers left Ireland "with shame on account of it" (*MG* 3). When Padden notices that Jaymony has returned to the loft, he is "the villain of the world, it's now he has us scandalised" (*MG* 15). We have already noted the infamy accorded Roger's house: "in a manner the childer go a mile . . . to avoid it" (*DD* 31). In *The Pie-Dish,* Margaret complains of the "family being made a hambug of over that old pie-dish" (*P-D* 48–49). When Leum dies, having refused to take last rites, Johanna laments that "it's disgraced we'll be over him during the duration of time through the length and breadth of Europe" (*P-D* 56).

But this superficial threat of social ostracism masks a far more deep-seated fear of the artist and the power of his art. Johanna claims Margaret's dislike of scandal is just an excuse, rightfully asserting, "It's in dread of him you are, Mage" (*P-D* 49). Regarding the pie-dish, the usually irreverent and sarcastic Jack ultimately senses "it's in dread I am of it" (*P-D* 46).

At the root of this "dread" lies the double-edged response noted earlier: art and artist may be condemned as pagan, haunted, and ineffectual, but their power must be respected, for the essential fear underlying this aggression is that these loonies may in fact be in control of a higher, more divine knowledge than the community can comprehend. Enid Welsford reminds us,

> There is a widespread notion which is not yet quite extinct that the lunatic is an awe-inspiring figure whose reason has ceased to function normally because he has become the mouthpiece of a spirit, or power external to himself, and so has access to hidden knowledge. . . .[14]

If Roger is but a "looney fool," why do representatives of the church, family and two contentious factions of the Other-world scrap so desperately for his dolls? Leum's "prancing about the floor with the eyes lepping out of his head" (*P-D* 46) unites the defiant lunatic and his hauntingly obscure art with the pagan supernatural powers associated with traditional Irish artists. The community *imagines* that the artist possesses supernatural knowledge and power; it does not need objective evidence.

Given Fitzmaurice's treatment of art, artist, and community, the conflict in these plays is quite unlike that found in Yeats, Synge, and Colum. Further, the relation between conflict and resolution is equally dissimilar. The flaws in most criticism of Fitzmaurice result from an inability to locate and describe this difference. It is precisely in the relation between conflict and resolution that Fitzmaurice is unique—and most problematic. In describing the factors which affect conflict and resolution in his plays, we discover that what is at issue in the plays of Yeats, Synge, and Colum does not directly concern Fitzmaurice at all.

A major factor contributing to the peculiar conflict in Fitzmaurice's plays is that, unlike Seanchan, Conn, and Christy, Fitzmaurice's heroes cannot be separated from their art.[15] The source of the community's fear is not art or artist but the irrational obsession which fuses them. This intense, solipsistic fusion is their point of attack.

In response to this attack, the artist uses his artwork to divorce himself from the community. This obsession allows him to be: an artist creating (by some wayward aesthetic) his masterpiece; a visionary seeing in his art unfulfilled dreams and ambitions; or a good-for-nothing loafer preferring eccentricity to the tedium of a workaday existence. So the artwork could be art, or a goal which sets the eccentric visionary above his neighbors, or a drug to escape what Jaymony calls "being in the slush."[16] Significantly, though

these possibilities do not function simultaneously, they all
serve to separate the world of artist and society.

The dissociation of these two worlds results not from a
simple divergence of opinion and belief; in effect, the two
levels of consciousness which abide within Fitzmaurice's
stage world represent such a dislocation of sensibility and
worldview that Roger's doll shop and Jaymony's loft may as
well be Tír na nÓg itself. Consequently, a difficulty sur-
rounds any attempt to define an actual conflict in these plays
similar to those which are clearly evident in *The Fiddler's
House, The King's Threshold,* and *Playboy*. The characters in
Yeats, Synge, and Colum all live in one world. Consequently, the issues in conflict—land and family obligations
(for instance) versus artistic freedom—are understood by
both sides because they have an absolute, objective value. The
King, for example, comprehends why Seanchan values the
"ancient right of the poets," but he attributes less value to
that custom.

Because of its objective nature, conflict is revealed through
a series of either/or propositions and resolved by a choice
between them. Pegeen must decide, for instance, between the
visions of life represented by alliance with either Shawn or
Christy. Conn must either stay on the land with his family or
take to the road. Seanchan either dies with dignity or lives
with the awareness of his own complicity and compromise.
In Fitzmaurice's works, the difficulty in labeling the conflicts
results precisely from the absence of any possible ameliorative
choices. Fitzmaurice's artists and the community around
them share little or no common ground, and therefore rational either/or propositions cannot exist and no decisions
based upon the circumstances of the play will in fact resolve
the conflict which seems to be implied by the juxtaposition of
artist and community.

Why is this problem not simply solved by taking the view
of most critics that the conflict is essentially paganism vs.
Christianity?[17] Because the resolution that evolves from such

a conflict leads us to an indefensible and illogical conclusion: since the values and belief of Fitzmaurice's particular form of paganism are obscure beyond comprehension, the only values accessible to us are those of the community. If this is Fitzmaurice's "meaning," then the conflict becomes even more enigmatic by the total absence of anything we may objectively attribute to this paganism. Consequently, for both community and critics, paganism becomes a matter of deportment: Fitzmaurice's plays then become condemnations of ill–mannered loafers masquerading as artists and the community arises as the bastion of Christian belief in action.[18]

Do these extravagant fantasies ultimately support a cabbage-haggard conservatism? No. The bearers of these values are themselves ridiculous and ineffectual hypocrites. The debate between Padden and Maineen, which opens *The Magic Glasses* establishes their suspiciousness, pettiness, and gullibility, and prepares us to see in Quille nothing but a blunderbuss and a quack. Father Troy's quickness to pronounce Leum "dead, and . . . damned" establishes the limitations of his perspective. The community's social rituals are equally false and ineffective. Father James defends the dandy doll (and hence his geese) from the Hag's Son:

> Here, hold that gun, till I make the sign of the cross, read from the book, and drive that Hag's Son up the chimley in one mortal flame of fire. (Reads from book.) You won't go up the chimley, you won't? Let us see what will come of a clout of a fist. (Makes at Hag's Son and misses him) [DD 35]

Earlier he baptizes the doll, making it "sanctified and sacramental sound" in "holy armour" (*DD* 33) to escape the Barna Brat's power. Morgan Quille's sacramental pronouncement is an Irish stew of misbegotten phrases: "Sacramento, Dominus vobiscum, mea culpa, mea maxime culpa, kyrie eleison, excelsior!" (*MG* 10). Clearly these silly people cannot be the playwright's raisonneurs, the mouthpieces of his "meaning." But if they are petty, ineffectual, and superstiti-

ous, and if the artist's solipsism and subjectivity do obscure
the values represented by the artist and his art, where must we
look for meaning in these plays?

An accurate approach to Fitzmaurice's dramas requires that
we relinquish the notion that these works are about such
value–laden conflicts as "paganism vs. Christianity"; the
reader must see through this camouflage of work ethic,
church, family obligation, and personal character. The author
merely uses this superficial conflict to address an entirely
different subject—imagination itself.

To understand Fitzmaurice's treatment of the imagination,
we must look again at the artwork itself, particularly at what
happens to it as the play concludes. Unlike fiddle music and
poetry, Fitzmaurice's art is not independent of the artist; it is
fragile and impermanent. In each play not only does the artist
die (or disappear) but his work of art also disintegrates.[19]
These incidents are essential elements of the dramatic structure informing each play: a growing "conflict"—which is in
fact only the community attacking a strange artist—concludes
with the explosion of the artwork and the death or disappear-
ance of its creator.

This particular dramatic structure—especially the relation
of the resolution of the foregoing conflict—drastically separates Fitzmaurice from his contemporaries. The resolutions of
The King's Threshold, The Fiddler's House, and *Playboy* all
directly relate to the conflict and in effect resolve and comment upon it. This commentary often leaves the artist's
audience looking dull, reactionary, and dangerously
shortsighted. In *The King's Threshold,* the Mayor "never
understood a poet's talk" (*KT* 78); the Monk ably represents
the communal fear of "the wanton imagination of the poets"
(*KT* 81). The artist, they contend, ignores King and Church
and thus threatens rational order: "He is a man that hates
obedience,/ Discipline, and orderliness of life" (*KT* 84).
Consequently, when Seanchan dies an order is restored, but

we realize what the community has lost and the consequent pettiness that this order affirms.

Though the conclusions of *The Fiddler's House* and *Playboy* are more ambiguous, the same dynamics obtain: the unfulfilled artist is opposed by a reactionary community. Christy's actions, too, threaten order, and he and his father must be excluded from the community. Though their future is left uncertain, we know the artist's place is not the Mayo pub. Colum's fiddler does not find the community vicious and shortsighted, but simply lifeless and devoid of imagination: "People . . . would leave the best fiddler at the fair to go and look at a bullock" (*FH* 11). Thus Colum's conclusion links Conn's flight to Christy's in that both set out in quest of an audience who are neither fools nor dullards. The artist, representing an anarchical and pagan imagination dedicated to freedom and independence of mind, is countered by his stage audience: conservative, suspicious of the irrational, and devoted to an order stabilized by obligations to work, family, and the Catholic Church.

Fitzmaurice's resolutions do not directly comment upon the conflict. Neither Leum's death nor the breaking of the pie-dish is caused by his antagonists. Roger is swept away by forces from another world; Cauth and Father James remain as ineffectual and mystified as ever. Jaymony's case is again more complex. He dances until "the house is creaking" and employs his magic to rivet his pursuers to the loft ladder. Because he returns to the loft only after he learns his despised brothers have returned, and because Jaymony has never before performed his frantic *jig macabre* or used his power directly on the community, we sense he has no further alternatives: he intends this ascent to be his last. Thus his death represents an apocalyptic self–transcendence, which *he* controls, not Padden, Maineen, and company. Therefore, their antagonism only indirectly affects the conclusion.

These disintegrative finales fail to shed light on the identity

of the artist or the nature of his now-destroyed art. Though
Conn and Christy sever their communal identity, they gain
an identity within a larger community of wandering poets and
musicians. Though like Fitzmaurice's heroes, Seanchan dies,
his pupils insure that his identity as poet will endure. In
contrast, we can only associate Fitzmaurice's naturals with a
solipsistic obsession and an obscure connection to the
Otherworld, both of which remain mysterious to the end.
Here the distinction between artist and natural becomes
essential: Conn, Christy, and Seanchan are conscious of
themselves as artists and therefore can articulate a viable
argument against their antagonists. Fitzmaurice's naturals
lack such self–consciousness, champion no causes, and
therefore present no argument. The conflict—at least on an
issue-oriented level—remains unbalanced and insubstantial.

In understanding the resolutions, the community's predict-
ably superstitious reactions are unhelpful. When art and artist
perish in death and disintegration, the community again
offers explanations that reaffirm its members' own "normalcy" and their vision of an ordered world. After Leum's
death, Father Troy condemns his "folly and vanity," and
pronounces him "dead, and . . . damned," while Margaret
prays for God's "mercy on his soul." They convert Leum's
obsession into denial of church doctrine. After Jaymony
dies, Padden and the rest stage an impromptu mock lament;
we see that the community is not above stretching the truth to
regain order.[20]

If the values of the community represent a fear–dominated
reliance upon irrelevant beliefs, and the values of the artist are
enshrouded in solipsism and other–worldliness, Fitzmaurice's
meaning resides elsewhere. It exists, rather, in the one point
of conjunction between artist and community—the
artwork—most specifically in the acts of imagination which
give it meaning. Because the artwork possesses no objective
value or significance, both sides project value on it, "imagine"
its meaning. Thus, the artist has no exclusive claim to the

powers of imagination. Every condemnation—every expression of communal belief—is in essence also an imaginative act. Both sides are obsessed: the artist's attachment to his artwork is no more excessive and irrational than the degree to which artist and art dominate the community's life and consciousness. Therefore, Fitzmaurice's central concern is not value and belief, but the fragility and abuse of imagination itself.

The community, confronted by the artwork and unable to understand it, exercises its traditional suspicion of the unfettered imagination and condemns the artist as a pagan and evil threat to its world. The people thus abuse the imagination by allowing it to distort and ignore the truth. The artist himself obviously exercises imagination in quite another manner: to separate himself—physically, intellectually, and spiritually—from the community. Potentially able to harness the imagination to create beauty, he instead buries himself and his work in solipsism, aggressively denying his public function and, most importantly, denying his art any relation to the objective world.

Though Fitzmaurice and his contemporaries share the same theme—the separation of the artist from Irish society—their points of attack are essentially and significantly different. Yeats, Synge, and Colum question those social values which force the artist into exile; their concern is essentially social. Fitzmaurice attacks this problem at the level of imagination itself. He is not directly concerned with the quality of society, but with the quality and function of imagination in a world which cannot accept its artists: society and artist each hide behind impenetrable masks—one of reactionary belief, the other of impotence and solipsistic fantasy.

Though Fitzmaurice's works are delightful exhibitions of truly original genius, a morbid distrust of this playwright's greatest asset—his imagination—lurks beneath every exorbitant line. This distrust gradually became a theme in Fitzmaurice's life as well as his art. Though his early play, *The Country Dressmaker* (1907), was a regular in the Abbey repertory for many years, and *The Pie-Dish* found a small following on a London tour, *The Magic Glasses* was condemned as "the silliest production ever attempted on the Abbey stage,"[21] and *The Dandy Dolls*, probably Fitzmaurice's most extraordinarily theatrical play, did not grace the Abbey boards until 1969, six years after the playwright's death. With few exceptions, his other plays suffered similar neglect.[22] Meanwhile, the small, reclusive bachelor labored as a low-ranking clerk for the Office of Agriculture until his retirement at 65. For two more decades he kept largely to himself, seldom venturing out in public except for an occasional stout in the basement of Mooney's. Though he remained a devotee of the music hall, we have no evidence that he saw a legitimate play—not even his own—during the last forty years of his life.

His later plays reflect this cynicism: after 1920, they contain no more artists, no more works of art. Instead, we find Martineen Collopy in *The Green Stone* (1925), who uses the stone's immense power to conjure large amounts of gold, useless because it floats away. In *The Linnaun Shee* (1924), farmer Jamesie Kennelly gives up his land and family to go with the Linnaun Shee, "a horrid wrinkled old hag." But the hag rejects him, and he returns, no longer moonstruck and fanciful, but industrious and rather bland in his dedication to family and work. These heroes are either incapable of inspired belief or shamelessly willing to pervert their power for material gain.

At their center, *The Pie-Dish*, *The Magic Glasses*, and *The Dandy Dolls* evade and confound us as readily as the artworks contained in them. Further, Fitzmaurice's world, when stripped of its enchanting language and dream-like surrealism, harbors no communication, justice, or love. Those apocalyptic resolutions deny us any belief that what came before them is worth any more than the lackluster company left behind. Fitzmaurice's plays—like the artists and artworks within them—seem created to self-destruct; they leave us charmed but empty-handed and uninspired. But these feelings should not diminish our estimation of this playwright and his contribution to Irish dramatic literature. In seeing the victim of the separation of artist and society to be not one or the other, but the imaginative and creative capacities of both, Fitzmaurice gives us a remarkably original and compelling vision of Irish life. We agree that these plays are "mysterious surely and fantastic strange," but Leum's erudite, crippled grandson has the last line:

"There, it's in bits now, and what it was or what it wasn't no one in the wide world will be a pin's point the wiser for ever more" (*P-D* 56).

NOTES

1. J. E. Caerwyn Williams, *The Court Poet in Medieval Ireland* (London: Oxford University Press, 1971), pp. 40, 22.

2. O. J. Bergin, "Bardic Poetry," *Journal of the Ivernian Society* 5 (1913): 154.

3. Williams, *The Court Poet*, p. 33. See also: Fred Norris Robinson, *Satirists and Enchanters in Early Irish Literature* (1911; reprint ed., in *Reprints in Irish Studies*, Vol. 1 [n.p.: American Committee for Irish Studies, n.d.]), pp. 97, 103; and Enid Welsford, *The Fool: His Social and Literary History* (London: Farrar and Rinehart, 1935), p. 89.

4. "The bardic profession was built upon the ruins of—or perhaps we might say was a protective metamorphosis of—the ancient druidic order, and was always a craft with its own dues, privileges and prerogatives, decided by itself" (Williams, *The Court Poet*, p. 2).

5. William Butler Yeats, *The King's Threshold*, in *The Collected Plays of W. B. Yeats* (New York: Macmillan Co., 1934), p. 72. Hereafter cited parenthetically in the text with the abbreviation *KT*.

6. J. M. Synge, *The Playboy of the Western World* (1907; reprint ed., New York: Barnes and Noble, 1969), p. 28. Hereafter cited parenthetically in the text with the abbreviation *PWW*.

7. Padraic Colum, *The Fiddler's House*, in *Three Plays* (Boston: Little, Brown, and Co., 1916), p. 29. Hereafter cited parenthetically in the text with the abbreviation *FH*.

8. According to Arthur E. McGuinness, a pie-dish is "more like what we would call a stew pot, a deep welled vessel for making meat pies" (*George Fitzmaurice*, Irish Writers Series [Lewisburg, Pa.: Bucknell University Press, 1975] p. 31).

9. George Fitzmaurice, *The Pie-Dish*, in *The Plays of George Fitzmaurice, Vol. II: The Folk Plays*, ed. Howard K. Slaughter (Dublin: Dolmen Press, 1969), p. 56. Hereafter cited parenthetically in the text with the abbreviation *P-D*.

10. George Fitzmaurice, *The Dandy Dolls,* in *The Plays of George Fitzmaurice, Vol. I: Dramatic Fantasies,* ed. Austin Clarke (Dublin: Dolmen Press, 1967), p. 22. Hereafter cited parenthetically in the text with the abbreviation *DD. The Magic Glasses* is in the same volume, and will be cited parenthetically in the text with the abbreviation *MG.*

11. Austin Clarke, Introduction to *Dramatic Fantasies,* p. xii.

12. Christy, too, asserts he "won't be the like of the clumsy young fellows do be ploughing all times in the earth and dung" (*PWW* 36).

13. We do not know, as J. D. Riley contends we do, that Leum wants "the fanciest play-and-putty pie dish in the world," nor can the text support his contention that the pie-dish "is to represent all the meaning and beauty of Leum's earlier and happier life" ("The Plays of George Fitzmaurice," *The Dublin Magazine* 31 (January-March 1955): 8–9. Several others make similar statements: Irving Wardle, "Reputations—XV: George Fitzmaurice," *The London Magazine* n.s. 4 (February 1965): 71; Gordon G. Erikson, "The Wonderful and the Probable in the Plays of George Fitzmaurice" (Ph.D. diss., University of Colorado, 1973), p. 122.

14. Welsford, *The Fool,* p. 76.

15. It thus seems impossible that any close reader can isolate this condemnation upon either art or artist separate from the other. Ignoring this, one critic claims that in *The Magic Glasses,* Fitzmaurice is "satirizing the uncreative visionary" (Nora M. Kelley, "George Fitzmaurice, 1877–1963: A Biographical and Critical Study" [Ph.D. diss., New York University, 1973], p. 145). Nothing in the play suggests that Jaymony's excessive strangeness would somehow cease or be excusable if he were to create something.

16. I am indebted to Carol Gelderman's analysis of *The Pie-Dish* in "In Defense of George Fitzmaurice" (Ph.D. diss., Northwestern University, 1972), pp. 137 ff.

17. See Andrew E. Malone, *The Irish Drama* (New York: Scribner's, 1929), p. 171; Ernest A. Boyd, *The Contemporary Drama of Ireland* (Boston: Little, Brown, and Co., 1917), p. 359; and McGuinness, *George Fitzmaurice,* p. 32.

18. Adopting this strategem, Riley asserts that Jaymony dies because he cannot give up his "dubious practices" ("The Plays of George Fitzmaurice," p. 9). John P. Conbere describes the artists as petty "bullying frauds and ineffectual dreamers" ("The Obscurity of George Fitzmaurice," *Eire-Ireland* 6, no. 1 [1971]: 23). Matthew Coughlin calls Jaymony a "false visionary" and says that the quack folk healer Quille is "our realist," and his absurd cure is "sound, temperate advice" ("Birth Astride a Grave: Theme and Structure in George Fitzmaurice's Dark Comedies" [Ph.D. diss., University of Iowa, 1975], pp. 93, 95).

19. Critics often either overlook or misinterpret these disintegrations. Indicative of such critical procedure is Austin Clarke's complaint that "the underlying tragedy of poverty and ignorance in *The Magic Glasses* is not really felt. This is due perhaps to the fact that the catastrophic ending . . . buries everything even deeper in a world of fantasy" (Introduction to *Dramatic Fantasies,* p. xii). Rather than grapple with such incongruity, Mr. Clarke chooses to complain that what is given him—a drama in which artists and artworks die—is not what he wishes to get—folk plays about Irish poverty and ignorance.

20. The resolutions often force critics and playgoing audiences to imitate these countryfolk and search through the remains for a statement confirming their own sense of order. Critical responses are often as value-loaded and desperate as Father Troy's. Matthew Coughlin comments on the conclusion of *The Magic Glasses:*

    . . . if we share Jaymony's dilemma, we cannot share his solution, seeing rather more clearly than he does that his fleeing to the loft creates, paradoxically, another world more grotesque, more desperate, more illusory than the one he simplistically seeks to avoid. ["Birth Astride a Grave," p. 103.]

Such words as "grotesque," "desperate," and "illusory" imply that if Jaymony could have undergone that marvellous cure, the conclusion should find him standing proudly beside his illustrious brothers, maybe someday becoming a "peeler" himself. Carol Gelderman asserts that because Fitzmaurice's artists "are not lonely heroes upholding a noble cause," they are "fools whose sacrifice is worthless" ("In Defense of George Fitzmaurice," p. 50). One infers that sacrifice has particular value in Fitzmaurice's world, and that nobility and heroics are at issue, neither of which is the case.

21. Joseph Holloway, quoted in *Joseph Holloway's Abbey Theatre: A Selection from His Unpublished Journal, "Impressions of a Dublin Playgoer,"* ed. Robert Hogan and Michael J. O'Neill (Carbondale, Ill.: Southern Illinois University Press, 1967), p. 157.

22. On Fitzmaurice's neglect, see Howard Slaughter, "Fitzmaurice and the Abbey," *Educational Theatre Journal* 22 (1970): 146–54; Gelderman, "Austin Clarke and Yeats' Alleged Jealousy of George Fitzmaurice," *Éire-Ireland* 8, no. 2 (1973): 62–70.

All Imaginable Things: Yeats's *Per Amica Silentia Lunae*

By Bryant E. Hoffman

Although *Per Amica Silentia Lunae* (1917) is most frequently looked upon as an "alphabet" for *A Vision,* the essay makes an important statement in its own right about the processes by which Yeats created poetry. In both form and content, *Per Amica* establishes the intellectual and spiritual construct by which the poet makes his seemingly personal, individual lyric poems an expression of a universal, tragic art. The doctrine of *Per Amica Silentia Lunae* provides its author with a mythology upon which to build his own poetic personality; the life of the poet is recreated as poetic subject, and biography thereby becomes a form of mythology.[1] The effects of this development are clearly seen in *The Wild Swans at Coole* (1919). In this volume, Yeats's voice for the poet reflects what at first seems to be a simple paradox: the first–person speaker takes on the objective quality of myth, while the third–person poets become intensely personal voices. The speaker of such a poem as "The Wild Swans at Coole," for example, becomes a mythological *persona* for a created personality of the poet, while Aherne and Robartes become mouthpieces for personal utterance.

The following discussion examines *Per Amica* as a statement of aesthetics directly effecting Yeats's poetry, particularly *The Wild Swans at Coole* (1919). However esoteric its content may seem to be, Yeats is using the essay to explain the basic principles upon which his poetry rests. A study of the essay shows clearly that by 1917 Yeats has found what to him is a justifiable means of formulating an artisitic unity based upon the opposition between his personality and its opposite, the anti–self. Yeats's essay also begins to explain the means by which he understood the mind of a great poet such as Dante who uses the struggle between himself and his Daimon as an expression of the duality of the universe of matter and spirit. If the poet—namely, Yeats himself—may come to see as the subject for his work a search for a Unity of Being in the internal struggle between self and Daimon, such a struggle may serve as an expression of the battle between *"Anima Hominis"* and *"Anima Mundi,"* the natural and spiritual worlds. Thus art will be the vehicle for an expression of the ultimate realization that the natural mirrors the spiritual as the individual mirrors his Daimon, and thereby personal utterance can mirror universal truth, and universal truth, personal utterance.

In the version published in 1917, *Per Amica Silentia Lunae* consists of five parts: a short prologue and an epilogue addressed indirectly to Iseult Gonne, "Ego Dominus Tuus," *"Anima Hominis,"* and *"Anima Mundi."* The major parts of the essay—*"Anima Hominis"* and *"Anima Mundi"*—are framed and held within both a personal and poetic framework which will be seen to complement their central thesis.

In the short "Prologue" addressed to "Maurice," Yeats suggests that the essay to follow will serve to complete a conversation between them "upon certain thoughts so long habitual that I may be permitted to call them my convictions."[2] The personal tone is established by reference to the fact that such serious conversation has been "often interrupted" and last interrupted by Iseult's black Persian cat, Minnaloushe, and his preference for stalking the brambles.

The mixing of what is trivial and personal with what is crucial and important is revealing here—the paragraph ends with the following two sentences:

> When I came back to London my mind ran again and again to those conversations and I could not rest till I had written out in this little book all that I had said or would have said. Read it some day when 'Minnaloushe' is asleep. [319]

The pursuit of the ideas that possess the poet must necessarily wait upon the cat's being asleep; what Yeats "had said" or what he "would have said," had circumstances permitted, describes the ambivalence and duality of tone. The trivial and the monumental come together in the paragraph and oppose each other.

Similarly, the "Epilogue" mixes trivia and significant statement as Maurice is told what Mallarmé had written in reference to the time of Yeats's youth—" 'All our age is full of the trembling of the veil of the Temple' "—(367) and then is shown the errors into which Yeats's generation fell: Strindberg occupies himself looking for the philosopher's stone and a young student has a ring made by "a Jewish Rabbi, of alchemical gold." The veil of the Temple did not rend itself in twain, and Yeats reveals his participation in the delusions of the time by saying, "My critical mind—was it friend or enemy?—mocked, and yet I was delighted" (367). The paragraph ends with a reiteration of the final error, both aesthetic and personal, into which Yeats conceived himself falling in the 1890s, but from which he has resurrected Axel's statement, " 'As for living, our servants will do that for us' " (368). While he still admires this line, the life–art controversy of the 1890s and Yeats's reflection of it in the poetry he wrote during that period are put in perspective here. Whereas earlier Yeats could find no means of reconciling the processes of life and the creation of art, *Per Amica* now presents a means by which the opposition between life and art is contained and transcended.

The doctrinal poem "Ego Dominus Tuus" follows the "Prologue" immediately and acts as an introduction to and summary of "*Anima Hominis,*" which follows it. The poem conveniently explicates by means of a dialogue between Hic and Ille the central issues informing the essay: it directly argues "the conflict between Self and Anti-Self, between perfection of life and work"[3] by propounding the doctrine of the "double" for which Ille speaks. Hic is obviously used to present ideas which Ille may then argue against by offering a rationale for his opposition, and thus the structure of the poem acts as an example of the kind of opposition which is its theme. Hic counsels Ille to find his style by "sedentary toil/And by the imitation of great masters," (323), but Ille argues that his style may only be formulated by pursuing the "Magical shapes" (321) in the sand beside the stream at Thoor Ballylee and by searching for the opposite to all that he is, all that he has seen, all that he has written. When Hic says that "[he] would find [himself] and not an image," Ille counters with one of Yeats's favorite arguments. Ille argues that the search for the "self" has been the cause of the modern, fragmented, and self-conscious artist's becoming a "timid, entangled, empty and abashed" critic who can "but half create" (321) because he has only personality and not its opposite, and thus is without the internal tension of contained opposition necessary to great art.

Although Hic gives Dante and Keats as examples of artists who found themselves and who wrote about their joy of self-discovery in poetry, Ille makes these poets fit his theory of the Daimon, the anti-self: he argues that Dante's poetry is informed by the tension between his "lecherous life" and the "unpersuadable justice" (322) offered to him through Beatrice, and that Keats made "luxuriant song" (323) out of the dissatisfaction occasioned by his illness and poverty. In his interpretation of these poets, Ille speaks for Yeats's theory of aesthetics as it is applied to his own poetry; art can only be made from the internal struggle occasioned by the artist's search for his mask, his anti-self:

> Ille. Because I seek an image, not a book.
> Those men that in their writings are most wise
> Own nothing but their blind, stupefied hearts.
> I call to the mysterious one who yet
> Shall walk the wet sands by the edge of the stream
> And look most like me, being indeed my double,
> And prove of all imaginable things
> The most unlike, being my anti-self . . .
>   [324]

Here, Ille makes it clear that the standard for tragic art applied as much to Yeats and his search as it does to Dante or Keats and their expressions of the "tragic war" (322).

The antithesis that controls "Ego Dominus Tuus" is central to *"Anima Hominis"* and *"Anima Mundi."* These two major sections of the essay take the form of personal reverie in which the poet's experience and opinion expand to encompass the spiritual and universal world of man's experience; the focus is primarily on the process by which the artist sees himself constructing an art controlled by both the conflict between the personality of the poet and its opposite, and the opposition between the human world of experience and the supernatural world of spiritual existence. These two kinds of being are connected in the essay by defining and developing the relationship between anti-self (or mask) and Daimon. This idea is explored and supported by discussions of Dante and Keats, who act as "case studies" of the dual opposition Yeats sees as necessary to the creation of tragic art, and by reference to the "double war" (330), which he must struggle to maintain as a poet trying to present an integrated, tragic art in a fragmented twentieth century. The art of the essay rests in its statement of a formal, integrated aesthetic by means of a

seemingly informal, disconnected series of sections. Thus the
two parts of *Per Amica Silentia Lunae* together act as an
example of the fusion of personal reverie and formal aesthetic.

In *"Anima Hominis"* the poet is presented as he who
creates art out of a constant conflict between his "heterogeneous and confused" (335) life and the ideal which he imagines
for himself. Unlike the saint, who achieves unity by contemplation, and the hero, who achieves it by action, the poet's
Unity of Being is achieved only in his art and is based upon
the internal war between contemplation and action. He consciously looks for and assumes a mask so that he may lose
"the infinite pain of self-realisation" (334) and find a means of
transforming into a unified art the contest between the incongruity, disappointment, and pain of his life, and the ideal
which he imagines. The mask, "the other self, the anti-self or
the antithetical self, as one may choose to name it, comes but
to those who are no longer deceived, whose passion is reality"
(331), and it is the means by which the poet creates the quarrel
within himself out of which poetry may be made. The creator
in this century must turn "from the mirror to meditation
upon a mask" (334), and from such a meditation and the
opposition it occasions comes the vitality upon which great
art has always depended.

But the simple turning from mirror to mask involves more
than at first seems evident. What exactly does Yeats mean by
defining the artist as he who is "no longer deceived, whose
passion is reality," and how does the artist reflect such a
"reality" in his work? Although the implications of these
questions are complex and demand a full examination of the
essay, a few "working definitions" may be appropriate here,
since in his essay Yeats has the habit of assuming a number of
different perspectives simultaneously. In Yeats's view, the
artist's work centers finally upon himself, and his reality is
finally a personal, subjective, and aesthetic one. But the "self"
that the artist assumes in his own work is an aggregate
expression of a Unity of Being, composed of a series of

antinomies, which create dramatic tension within the work itself. In this created, aesthetic unity, the figure of the artist (or poet) extends itself into all that it experiences and all that it can imagine. The artist finds in his work (or does it find him?) a hall of mirrors which, instead of distorting his image, clarifies and extends it.

The poet begins the process of creation with faith, "the highest achievement of the human intellect, the only gift man can make to God" (332), and only when he perceives the active existence of a spiritual world *(Anima Mundi)* beyond his conscious and subconscious mind can he make "real" art. The power of that world comes to him in dream, in vision, in what Yeats calls his creative "ecstasy." But although he must be aware of a spiritual power beyond his own artistic power, he can not totally give himself to it, because he must maintain his physicality, his sensuality by recognizing "the five/That make the muses sing," and he must study the ability of his own creative intellect to maintain both his physical sensuality and his spiritual faith so that he may record in his work the tension between them. Yeats's treatment of this highly abstract, yet sensual and personal, idea in section V of *"Anima Hominis"* confirms his commitment to both what is spiritual and what is physical: here he discusses poetry as "the quarrel with ourselves" (331), a quarrel exemplified with the intermingling of words suggesting physicality ("shudders," "passion," "ecstasy") within a definition of art as faith, as religion. The poet's created, aesthetic reality is greater than both the spiritual reality informing it and the mundane, physical reality in which he lives.

In other words, Yeats creates the figure of the poet as a symbol constructed from a series of irreconcilable oppositions. To make himself the theatre in which the necessary war informing poetic creation may be fought, the poet must meditate on a mask. The mask in *Anima Hominis* is an expression of the Daimon in *Anima Mundi*, and paradoxically it is the Daimon who brings man "to the place of choice"

(361) where he realizes his full freedom in the assumption of a fated mask. Although Yeats's argument in *Per Amica Silentia Lunae* is hard to follow and almost impossible to reconstruct, a certain amount of exposition will be necessary to explore the relationship between mask and Daimon and to show the importance of that relationship in Yeats's poetry.

Per Amica Silentia Lunae explores the idea that everything in the natural world *(Anima Hominis)* has its counterpart in the spiritual world *(Anima Mundi),* and by means of this correspondence, life becomes for Yeats a duality of experience which depends upon both the living and the dead, the natural and the supernatural, waking and dreaming, for animation and meaning. Although at one point he reflects that he had once thought of *Anima Mundi* as "a Great Memory passing from generation to generation" (345), the evidence he here pieces together from "old women in Connacht, mediums in Soho" (343), spiritualism, Henry More and the Cambridge Platonists, Spenser, Heraclitus, and his own experimentation suggests that the world of the dead, the world of the spirit, is far more active, more animate, more instructive than he had realized. Both the soul and the mind become the vehicles for *Anima Mundi:* the soul gives "substance to its images in the faint materialisation of our common thought" (350), and thus "mental images [become] no less than apparitions" (352). In fact, Yeats does not distinguish between a material reality, an intellectual or imagined one, and a spiritual one, and the aesthetic reality which he creates in his art is based upon this "conceptual unity," formulated by a process which is simultaneously sensual, mental, and spiritual. As a prelude to the artistic construct he creates in the poetry, this kind of unity makes it possible—indeed, fated—for the poet to create in his *persona* an instrument to assert simultaneously the personality's search for its anti-self in *Anima Mundi* and the processes of that search. The poet's mind becomes a force which binds the poetry together in a Unity of Being; that Unity, in asserting its own process, confirms the existence of an aggregate reality composed of flesh and spirit. Lest all of this sound like the high Germanic literary criticism of the late nineteenth century (the abstract nature of which Yeats no doubt would have disapproved), a sensible definition of the idea may be given by jumping ahead to a passage in *On the Boiler*. Yeats asserts directly here that space (and necessarily the material objects in it) was in antiquity part of man's mind, just as his mind was a mere extension of his progressive, reincarnate soul. And to express such a construct, only metaphor will do:

> I want to make my readers understand that explanations of the world lie one inside another, each complete in itself, like those perforated Chinese ivory balls.[4]

To give all of these "explanations of the world" simultaneously, to express all of "those perforated Chinese ivory balls" in all their intricate beauty is to create an aesthetic reality, a Unity of Being.

If, as Yeats says, the dead can only "free themselves from an endless sequence of thoughts" (353–54) by communication with and direction of the human soul and mind, the living can only "free themselves from an endless sequence of objects" (353) by cultivating the processes of dream, reverie, and vision which are necessary to the manifestation of *Anima Mundi* to the living person (343–48). If the person is an artist and can learn that all "mental images [are] no less than apparitions" (352), he comes to realize that "it is possible through a proper understanding and control of natural objects or symbols to invoke the spiritual and eternal world,"[5] and that his battle to create and realize the mask as a necessary opposite to his identity is actually a struggle to reflect in this "internal war" the duality of the natural and spiritual world which is the foundation of his art.

Yeats symbolizes these two counterparts of "reality" as, respectively, "the terrestrial and the condition of fire" (356), and the soul can only integrate them or become fully aware of their duality when "sequence comes to an end, time comes to an end" (357). Meanwhile, the soul "must fix its attention upon what is near, thinking of objects one after another" (358) and communicate with *Anima Mundi* "through the association of thoughts or images or objects" (359). It is through such an association that the dead, who reflect the Condition of Fire, may reveal themselves to the mind, which reflects the terrestrial condition.

If the dead of *Anima Mundi* may reveal to a living man the duality of existence through his receptive mind, they in turn receive "their mirrored life" from the Condition of Fire. If man's mind receives the reflection of the Condition of Fire from the dead, Yeats says that such a revelation is received "upon the winding path called the Path of the Serpent" (361), but if his soul passes "for a lengthy or a brief period out of the mirror life, as we in sleep out of the bodily life" (361), he may pass directly to an intellectual revelation from the Condition of Fire, and this revelation "falls principally upon straight paths" (361):

> In so far as a man is like all other men, the inflow finds him upon the winding path, and in so far as he is a saint or sage, upon the straight path. [361]

At this point in *"Anima Mundi"* Yeats turns to a consideration of the Daimon. The Daimon is one of the dead of *Anima Mundi,* and as such he reveals to the man "like all other men" the reflection of a mirrored life from the Condition of Fire upon a winding path, but he has the power to reveal to the saint or sage the Condition of Fire upon the straight path also: his power, says Yeats, is "zigzag, illuminating the passive and active properties" (361). Because the artist is both active and contemplative, partaking of the qualities of both saint and sage, the Daimon can not be escaped. He "brings man again and again to the place of choice, heightening temptation that the choice may be as final as possible, imposing his own lucidity upon events, leading the victim to whatever among works not impossible is the most difficult" (361); the Daimon "shapes into its own image the antithetical dream of man or nation" (362). That which "knits" together the Daimon and the man is the mask which permits "the expression of all the man most lacks, and it may be dreads, and of that only" (335).

Thus through the action of the Daimon, a man is brought paradoxically to the choice of a mask which is an expression of all he lacks and all he dreams. His choice of a mask is, however, now more than a contained opposition between himself and his anti–self: it becomes a dynamic and fated choice which involves the spiritual world, the Condition of Fire, inextricably within the material world, the terrestrial condition. Finally, when it is remembered that the assumption of the mask is for Yeats necessary to the creation of an unfragmented art, poetry necessarily is dependent upon the action of the Daimon, upon the fusion of the natural and spiritual, the temporal and universal. The artist not only celebrates the conflict between self and mask, but the extension of that conflict into an external world of the spirit. Yeats has constructed an aesthetic which expands the internal duality of man's struggle with his opposite into a total duality of existence, which includes all matter and spirit, all space and time.

Such an abstract and complex theory of creation is made more immediate and palatable in *Per Amica Silentia Lunae* by Yeats's citing of poets who, at least in his view, act as examples for the abstract theories he propounds. Harold Bloom calls our attention to the dependence of the abstract argument here upon such poets as Wordsworth, Blake, Shelley, Keats, and Spenser, but notes the hesitancy of Yeats in using himself as an example of his own theory. After suggesting that Yeats is careful about "identifying himself with his anti–self, of being made one with his own phantasmagoria," Bloom argues that in his discussions of Dante and

Shelley, "Yeats returns to the true depths of his own *antithetical* conception. . . ."[6] While it is quite true that Yeats depends upon reference to other poets to support the central abstraction the essay maintains, he does not seem to be hesitant about involving himself in the argument. In fact, Yeats's use of himself as exemplifying the aesthetic doctrines of *Per Amica* is quite evident. *"Anima Hominis"* begins with two paragraphs which present in the first person a focus upon the central antithesis which the rest of the essay explicates. While the third paragraph reveals that the title of the preceding poem ("Ego Dominus Tuus") is from Dante's vision of the "Lord of Terrible Aspect," it might be remembered that *"Anima Mundi"* ends with another "chamber" scene, but there the vision is Yeats's, not Dante's.

Yeats moves in the second section of *"Anima Hominis"* from the opposition within himself to a consideration of the opposition between life and art as presented by writers whom he has known well: Synge, for example, while resisting death personally, gives to Deirdre an acceptance of death (328). Section III expands the idea to include "any great poetical writer of the past" whose writing shows "that the work is the man's flight from his entire horoscope, his blind struggle in the network of the stars" (328). Then follow Morris, Landor, Keats, and in the next section Dante as examples. Dante is given much discussion since, as we have seen earlier, Yeats looks upon him as one of the past poets who was able to turn "from the mirror to meditation upon a mask" and by so doing present for Yeats an integrated poetry reflective of the "double war" within himself and with the images of *Anima Mundi*. Postulating such a conflict in Dante's art is obviously a means of explicating the opposition within his own poetry.

Next come in *"Anima Hominis"* an abstract, almost doctrinal series of statements which draw contrasts between rhetoric and poetry and their subjects, between the saint and hero as opposed to the poet, and between the modern and Renaissance worlds. But Yeats turns then to a series of

personal statements before proceeding to the Daimon and its
relationship to the destiny of man. For example:

> I find in an old diary: 'I think all happiness depends on the energy
> to assume the mask of some other life, on a re–birth as something
> not one's self, something created in a moment and perpetually
> renewed; in playing a game like that of a child where one loses the
> infinite pain of self–realisation, in a grotesque or solemn painted
> face put on that one may hide from the terror of judgement. . . .
> Perhaps all the sins and energies of the world are but the world's
> flight from an infinite blinding beam'. [334]

Notice here the tendency to turn personal reference into a
final abstraction of universal energy complete with the light
imagery Yeats will establish in "Anima Mundi" as the Condition of Fire.

References to old age and the necessity of maintaining
energy and renewed vision to avoid the fall of Landor or
Wordsworth are echoes at various places in Per Amica, and
certainly express an almost too personal context beneath the
dignity of the prose:

> A poet, when he is growing old, will ask himself if he cannot
> keep his mask and his vision without new bitterness, new disap-
> pointment. . . . Surely, he may think, now that I have found
> vision and mask I need not suffer any longer. . . . Then he will
> remember Wordsworth withering into eighty years, honoured
> and empty–witted, and climb to some waste room and find,
> forgotten there by youth, some bitter crust. [342]

"Anima Hominis" was dated February 25, 1917, and Yeats
was approaching his fifty-second birthday; his marriage did
not occur until November of the same year.

As the doctrines of "Anima Hominis" are partially explicated by personal reference, so "Anima Mundi" begins and
ends with Yeats himself as subject.[7] Before giving the abstract
definition and explanation of Anima Mundi, Yeats introduces
his own past experiences by which the spiritual world was

revealed to him, and he concludes the essay with two personal, subjective sections, which together summarize and focus the doctrines which have been examined:

> The books say that our happiness comes from the opposite of hate, but I am not certain, for we may love unhappily. And plainly, when I have closed a book too stirring to go on reading, and in those brief intense visions of sleep, I have something about me that, though it makes me love, is more like innocence. I am in the place where the Daimon is, but I do not think he is with me until I begin to make a new personality, selecting among those images, seeking always to satisfy a hunger grown out of conceit with daily diet; and yet as I write the word 'I select,' I am full of uncertainty, not knowing when I am the finger, when the clay. [365–66]

The essay concludes with a personal rendition of the explicated theory in operation, and throughout *Per Amica Silentia Lunae* Yeats does not hesitate to mix what is seemingly trivial with what is profound, and what is personal with what is abstract. These characteristics of the essay are in fact its very point: the "heterogeneous and confused" human condition is ennobled only in the face of the power and simplicity of the Daimon, and great tragic art is possible only when it reflects this central battle. As the natural and spiritual worlds are made of one world, so in microcosm are the self and the anti–self made one by opposition. This doctrine informs the ultimate paradox of Yeats's poetry: while his art seems to present the images of *Anima Mundi* as an ideal to be achieved at all costs and while the doctrine of the anti–self is presented as a positive means to achieve the ideal, spiritual reality of those images, the poetry in fact records and ennobles the contest between reality and dream. The artist, "whose passion is reality," may succumb neither to an ideal vision of reality nor to the trivial reality the mirror reflects back to him, for "reality" is the opposition between them, and that reality is tragic.

In the *Collected Poems, The Wild Swans at Coole* is dated 1919, although many of the poems included in and arranged for the section were written between 1915 and 1918.[8] John Unterecker argues that the volume is unified by its reflection of personal, national, and international events, and organized by a progression "from uncomplicated personal statement to an elaborate presentation of the intricate image on which *A Vision* is founded."[9] *The Wild Swans at Coole* is in many ways characterized by the progression which Unterecker summarizes: there is a recognizable difference between the first–person *persona* of "The Wild Swans at Coole," for example, and the *personae* to whom Yeats gives the visions and doctrinal wisdom of the final poems in the volume. But the progression of this group of poems is more complex than a movement from personal anecdote in the first person to doctrinal statements explicating Yeats's "system" by means of a third–person speaker. The poems, ostensibly personal *or* objective, are actually both personal *and* objective because they are informed by the correspondence between the material world of *Anima Hominis* and the spiritual world of *Anima Mundi* as explicated in *Per Amica;* they thus depend upon a duality in which what is physical and concrete becomes an expression of what is spiritual and abstract. Likewise, the *personae* in the poems intensify the duality between the physical and the spiritual and act as a means by which such a duality is focused and intensified; the *persona,* whether first person or third person, is subject to the same universal opposition as the poet who, to create great art, must meditate upon his opposite, his mask, as an image from the Daimon and thus from the spiritual world. Like the poet who creates a tragic art by "meditation on the mask" and by a reflection within his work of the internal opposition that creates it, the *personae* "must all find images—solid human images—to represent the reality that they cannot reach without some concrete embodiment."[10] Whether or not the poem is "spoken" in the first person or the third person, it must reflect the personal and universal duality of opposition which occasions its creation; there is no escape from the Daimon, for either the poet or the *personae* who speak his poems.

The theory of aesthetics Yeats develops in *Per Amica Silentia Lunae* not only defines his conception of his own poetry, but also describes the process inherent in the creation of all tragic art. By the very nature of the "argument" and the abstract "unity" it postulates, the theory must apply to the work of all great artists "whose passion is reality"; in fact, although the essay itself defines Yeats's conception of all art by frequent discussion of other poets (such as Dante, Keats, Wordsworth, etc.), it is fascinating that in the poems written after *Per Amica,* which have art as their central focus, Yeats frequently defines the processes of his own art by reference to specific works in several different media. Art objects such as Sato's sword, the Tower and its stair, Clifton's gift of a sculpture in lapis lazuli, and the statue of Cuchulain in the General Post Office become for Yeats a means of exemplifying the creations of the artist as concrete expressions of an aesthetic unity which is mythological and spiritual. All great art is infused, it seems, with the eternal forms of *Anima Mundi.* Again, we see Yeats extending his perception of his own theory so that it unifies the work of the generic "artist," and this is clearly to Yeats's advantage in creating an art which strives to express Unity of Being. But even if we do not accept Yeats's theory—if, that is, we lack what Yeats calls the artist's "faith"—there is another important way in which this aesthetic theory works to Yeats's benefit as an artist: it enables him to unite his study of the occult and his work as a poet. He does not have to give up one for the other, and he does not even have to declare a preference. The discipline, form, and structure of art become a testimony to the dream, the vision, the powerful supernaturalism to which he was committed. Yeats's "mysticism" becomes here a controlled mythology of aesthetics; and—whatever the dead may know or think—that aesthetic accommodates "perfection of the life" by making it

become "perfection of the work." The poet may *become* what
he creates.

NOTES

1. T. R. Henn, *The Lonely Tower: Studies in the Poetry of W. B. Yeats* (London: Methuen, 1950), p. 120.

2. W. B. Yeats, *Per Amica Silentia Lunae*, in *Mythologies* (New York: Macmillan Co., 1959), p. 319. All page references are to this edition and are hereafter cited parenthetically in the text.

3. Henn, *Lonely Tower*, p. 124.

4. W. B. Yeats, *On the Boiler* (Dublin: Cuala, 1939), p. 25.

5. Thomas Parkinson, *W. B. Yeats, Self-Critic: A Study of His Early Verse* (Berkeley and Los Angeles: University of California Press, 1951), p. 12.

6. Harold Bloom, *Yeats* (New York: Oxford, 1970), pp. 180–81.

7. T. S. Eliot, "Yeats," in *Yeats: A Collection of Critical Essays*, ed. John Unterecker (Englewood Cliffs, N.J.: Prentice-Hall, 1963), pp. 54–63. Although in his essay (delivered as the first annual Yeats Lecture in 1940), Eliot does not refer directly to *Per Amica* when he discusses Yeats's fusion of a personal and theoretical aesthetic, he clearly recognizes this characteristic in Yeats's work. After referring to his own idea of "impersonality in art" and saying that he "can never bear to reread" his own prose, Eliot comments as follows: "There are two forms of impersonality: that which is natural to the mere skilled craftsman, and that which is more and more achieved by the maturing artist. . . . The second impersonality is that of the poet who, out of intense and personal experience, is able to express a general truth; retaining all the particularity of his experience, to make of it a general symbol. And the strange thing is that Yeats, having been a great craftsman in the first kind, became a great poet in the second. It is not that he became a different man, for, as I have hinted, one feels sure that the intense experience of youth had been lived through— and indeed, without this early experience he could never have attained anything of the wisdom that appears in his later writing. But he had to wait for a later maturity to find expression of early experience; and this makes him, I think, a unique and especially interesting poet" (57). Although Eliot does not "dissimulate the fact that there are aspects of Yeats's thought and feeling" to which he is unsympathetic, particularly in regard to what he calls Yeats's "doctrine" (63), and although my discussion of Yeats's aesthetic in *Per Amica Silentia Lunae* does not directly depend upon Eliot's definition of Yeats's two forms of "impersonality," there is a definite recognition in Eliot's statement that Yeats's life and personality become a form of what he (Eliot) calls "impersonality."

8. A. Norman Jeffares, *A Commentary on the Collected Poems of W. B. Yeats* (Stanford, Calif.: Stanford University Press, 1968), p. 152.

9. John Unterecker, *A Reader's Guide to W. B. Yeats* (New York: Farrar, Straus, Noonday, 1959), p. 131.

10. George T. Wright, *The Poet in the Poem: The Personae of Eliot, Yeats, and Pound* (Berkeley and Los Angeles: University of California Press, 1960), p. 111.

Women, War, and Words: Frank O'Connor's First Confessions

By James H. Matthews

"The loneliest creature on God's earth is a young writer trying to find himself." By this observation about the tortures of his first two books, *Guests of the Nation* (1931) and *The Saint and Mary Kate* (1932), Frank O'Connor probably was referring to his fumbling search for a suitable literary style. What he neglected to add was that there is also nothing more lonely than a passionate and naive young man from a provincial town fumbling for a suitable social style in the big city. A self-taught amateur in all things, he simply improvised love as he had his education while fumbling for a literary style at the same time. It was the loneliest time of his life, a time spent vacillating between magical intensity and severe melancholy.

I

O'Connor's first published stories carried the weight of Daniel Corkery's influence. "Sion" and "The Peddler," for example, resembled in tone and theme the stories of *A Munster Twilight*, the book which in 1916 had triggered a revolution in the mind of young Michael O'Donovan— O'Connor's real-life counterpart.[1] Shortly after his release from prison, in the "first flush of remembrance," he began writing about his war experiences, mostly effusive poems but brief prose sketches as well. While serving as county librarian in Cork he tinkered with these sketches in the first of his writing journals. The approach was more reminiscent than thoughtful.

In prison O'Connor had listened carefully to fellow prisoners talk endlessly of their war experiences, mostly exaggerating them in the telling. He took bits and pieces of their anecdotes and forged them first into sketches, and eventually into short stories with dramatic pace and emotional clarity about simple people in not-so-simple situations. The stories had been knocking about in his mind for some time, gathering force and direction as he walked the wet streets of Cork. In Dublin he was free to work out some of those stories in his peripatetic and improvisational way. The flurry of activity from 1929 to 1930 when he wrote the stories of *Guests of the Nation* was characteristic of the way he approached every volume of stories he ever produced. He would write a story or two under some spontaneous spell and then begin to sense a larger picture, a set of stories, cohesively related by some thread or other. In a blaze of enthusiasm he would write more stories under the same voice. Then, frustrated by their crudity he would doggedly re-write the very stories that had generated the whole notion in the first place.

The fifteen stories which eventually came together in *Guests of the Nation* were conceived in O'Connor's mind as a unified volume, somewhat in the manner of Corkery's *A Munster Twilight* and Joyce's *Dubliners*, even more in the manner of George Moore's *The Untilled Field*, the book which he believed contributed a new simplicity of form and style to the prose fiction of the Irish literary movement. Based on Turgenev's *Sportsman's Sketches* Moore's volume of stories seemed to span, in the mind of the young Frank O'Connor, the gap between poetry and realism. He believed that Moore was trying to reach the essentials of prose fiction just as Yeats was trying to reach the essentials of drama. And just as it was Synge and O'Casey rather than Yeats who pointed the way to a viable realism in drama, it was inevitably Joyce not Moore who expressed the possibility of a realistic norm in fiction. Still, O'Connor always felt that Irish literature had produced no better single story than Moore's "Home Sickness."

The first three stories of *Guests of the Nation* concern the struggle with Britain—from the Easter Rising to the Treaty. The next eight stories deal exclusively with the Civil War, while the final four stories, which seem somewhat out of place, are set in ambiguous time before or after the times of violence and national upheaval. Offhandedly, O'Connor called it his "war book" in a letter to Nancy with an equally casual reference to Isaac Babel's *The Red Cavalry,* which had just been translated.[2] That Babel's stories made an impression on the young O'Connor is without question. He found them compelling in a disturbing way; he had been reading Russian fiction for some time, but this book spoke a new sensibility. Babel's war stories contained violence mingled with elegance and lyricism. "My First Goose" and "The Death of Dolgushov," two stories about the effect of outright brutality on sensitive individuals, undoubtedly touched a close nerve in O'Connor, whose own war memories still plagued him—not what had happened so much as how he had reacted. In Babel's stories he saw another way to span realism and poetry, to redirect intense moral concerns through stringent esthetic form. O'Connor was not so much influenced by the violence as by the manner of the stories—control, brevity, objectivity, and a lyrical apprehension of human problems.

Intense as his response to Babel was, O'Connor actually relied more heavily on another Russian for the conception of his own war stories. Turgenev's *Sportsman's Sketches* remained O'Connor's model for a volume of stories—each story discreet and whole, yet related by some thematic ambiance to the other stories in the volume. What unity *Guests of the Nation* possessed was more of tone than of theme, however, for inevitably O'Connor's mind gravitated from idea to situation, from theme to character. For a storyteller like O'Connor, life is a highly fragile and personal affair unified not by grand abstractions but by the inconvenient, elusive, and diverse patterns etched by common humanity across the surface of events. Invariably, his imagination forced itself through the picturesque, the historical, or the abstract to some situational flash point, some point of vivid impact where story becomes a "lyric cry in the face of destiny."

The violence and idealism of the events of 1916 to 1923 created in Ireland a mood of national hysteria. At least that was the voice heard by O'Connor trying to capture those events in prose six years after. In fact, the two extremes between which *Guests of the Nation* vacillates are hysteria and melancholy, between thoughtless act and numbed thoughtfulness. Benedict Kiely detected in these stories a "genuine bliss–was–it–in–that–dawn–to–be–alive romanticism," an adolescent enjoyment of the guns, the ambushes, the flying-columns. Indeed, this hysterical romanticism swirls across the surface of all but the last four stories.

"Jumbo's Wife," "Alec," and "Machine-Gun Corps in Action" are examples of the romanticized violence of the sort O'Connor found in Isaac Babel. In these stories war exposes the folly and weakness of character as well as the normal responses of people under pressure. Situation dominates character and the voice is blurred. The stories fail, not because O'Connor idealized violence, but because he failed to control its comic energy.

However, the next story in the volume, "Laughter," delivers a more clearly realized comic story from an equally absurd misadventure. Boys playing soldier find all the ingredients of a daring ambush—revolvers, Mills bombs, trenchcoats, and dark alleys. The story is the fictional account of the poem "Ambush," written in 1924 about the time O'Connor, Sean O'Faolain, Sean Henrick, and Vincent O'Leary

tried to sabotage a Free State convoy. After the explosion the
boys flee; in the "sweet sensation of flight" the main character, Stephen,

> heard beside him something that was like sobbing, the throaty
> sobbing of hysteria, and had almost given way to his surprise and
> consternation before he realised what it was. Not sobbing, but
> chuckling, a quiet contented chuckling, like a lover's laughter in a
> dark lane. In spite of himself he found the mirth contagious, and
> chuckled too. There was something strange in that laughter,
> something out of another world, inhuman and sprightly, as
> though some gay spirit were breathing through them both.[3]

At that instant O'Connor captures the human dimension of
the violence he has taken as his subject, the strange ways men
react to hazard and death. Situation reveals character and the
voice is momentarily clear. The playful and derisive laughter
which follows Alec's opening anecdote about a harelip gives
way to the uneasy laughter of hysteria.

However, in this story the hysteria is controlled; thematic
tragedy gives way to the comic twist of character. An old
woman emerges from "the gloom of an archway" and comes
toward the fleeing boys. Stanton and Nolan (Hendrick and
O'Faolain) continue but Cunningham and Stephen (O'Leary
and O'Donovan) stop to speak. "They were above the city
now, and it lay far beneath them in the hollow, a little bowl of
smudgy, yellow light." The old woman asks if it was shooting
she heard "below be the cross" (133). With "wild, happy
eyes" Cunningham replies that it wasn't shooting at all only a
deaf old woman in a shop below spending a winter night,
"blowing paper bags!" A laugh shakes her frail body and she
hails the "young devil" disappearing with his comrade "under
the gloom of the trees" (134). The laughter of this survivor
persists in the face of hysteria and gloom, the two extremes
between which young O'Donovan/O'Connor ran his course.

"Attack," the second story of the volume, was more than
likely written during the summer of 1929 before O'Connor's

holiday. If such stories as "September Dawn" and "Nightpiece with Figures" represent O'Connor's lyrical voice, then
"Attack" represents his objective, detached voice. It shows
especially how he built a story (or in those years improvised
one) not from an idea but from an incident. The attack of the
story provides the situation, the place and time, the reason for
the narrator and his comrade to be where they are. Two
young rebels intend to attack a police barracks two hours
after midnight. The ostensible enemy is the British, particularly the police who manned the garrisons tucked at the edge
of so many villages in West Cork. But the real enemies are
fear and loneliness with which the "peasants" in these isolated
pockets are forced to live. Since it is only nine when they
approach the area, they are obliged to take shelter in a nearby
farmhouse. At this point Lomasney tells Owen—who like
most of O'Connor's narrators is a good listener—a story
about the family living in the farmhouse ahead. It is a story
about a boy who loved a girl, struck and killed the "waster"
she was married to, and was sent off to America by his
friends. "We were frightened of the law in those days" (23),
Lomasney admits. That was five years before and no word
from Paddy since. The narrator observes that he was moved
by the tale mostly because it diverted his thoughts from the
barracks below.

Actually, in the diversion lies the gist of the story. The
atmosphere inside the cottage is what O'Connor is interested
in and not the mission of destruction. The two rebels are
intruders in the life of this Irish–speaking couple. During the
night they discover the source of old Kiernan's defensiveness
—Paddy, their son, hiding "bearded, emaciated, half-savage"
in the loft (31). Indeed the diversion becomes the story, not
as an unexpected twist or surprise but the unknown lurking
just below the surface of all human affairs. Had O'Connor
ended the story there it would have been merely a sentimental
story of coincidence. Instead he focuses his attention on
Lomasney who assumes command of the situation by in-

structing the old man to take the boy to the village and allow him simply to turn up. After the attack the police won't be worrying about him anyway. "That's what we're out for" (33). The story is neither about the attack nor the discovery of a boy but the passage to maturity achieved by Lomasney, hardly more than a boy himself.

As surely as violence and hysteria, along with their safety valve of comic hilarity, dominate the surface of *Guests of the Nation*, a more serious and thoughtful voice operates below that surface, a voice of compassion and bitterness. After all, war is not a normal situation, at least not for amateur warriors. The humor of "Laughter" and "Machine-Gun Corps in Action" is the comedy of disorder, of natural nervous tension in the face of violent death. O'Connor distrusted the cold, organizational mind of the professional soldier, for whom fear and disorder have been disciplined away. If romantic hysteria, nervous laughter, and chaotic fear represent natural responses of plain people to the stress of war, then disillusionment, accompanied by loneliness and melancholy, emerges just as naturally from the violence and stress. After "hysteria" the other word used throughout the volume more than might be normally expected is "melancholy."

Although *Guests of the Nation* carries no dedication (unlike the rest of O'Connor's books), it is most certainly for Sean Hendrick, by whose side O'Connor spent most of his battle time in 1921 and 1922, running dispatches for Erskine Childers and turning out publicity sheets on a commandeered printing press. War was a romance, a love affair for them both, second only to their love affair with language and literature. So O'Connor began writing his war stories to capture something of the romance and the agony of the whole affair. In May of 1929, O'Connor wrote a story (probably rewritten from an earlier Cork draft) entitled "September Dawn," which was given the inscription "To Sean Hendrick" when published in July in the *Dublin Magazine*. The story seems to crystallize those fundamental beliefs he had come to terms with in the Civil War, particularly his belief in the manifold richness of human life and his distrust of grand abstractions. It also represented a breakthrough in terms of technique, an indication of that delicate merging of romanticism and realism which gives his finest fiction a special edge. "September Dawn" is at once highly personal and severely objective.

"September Dawn" is the centerpiece of *Guests of the Nation* in the same way "Fugue" is the centerpiece of Sean O'Faolain's volume of stories, *Midsummer Night Madness*. Neither is the finest story of its volume but each is the emotional core and both are about the same set of events. O'Connor's letters to Nancy McCarthy at the time indicate that he and O'Faolain were still close yet still competitive.[4] O'Faolain wrote a wildly enthusiastic letter, commending the beauty of "Nightpiece" and "September Dawn," the two most lyrical stories in the book. O'Connor, in turn, defended Sean's volume of stories to Nancy, particularly "The Small Lady" and "Fugue," both of which combine adolescent vigor with melancholy rumination. Where O'Faolain treats a moment of love amidst the fear and loneliness of war through a highly descriptive first person narrative, O'Connor handles the same moment entirely from the outside. In both stories the darkness and the anxiety are given impressionistic shape, though for O'Faolain the idea is more cohesive because O'Connor is too easily diverted by character. Still, both stories end with a vague kind of hope in a rising morning.

"September Dawn" is the centerpiece of *Guests of the Nation* not for its theme but its voice. The lyricism of O'Connor's adolescent poems has by now been distilled into the poetic realism of a man looking back on the time of his passage to maturity. The romance of war with its tragic violence and comic disarray has been diverted to a melancholy acceptance of love and friendship. The hysteria of death has become the melancholy of life. The process of the boys in the story is the process reflected in the entire volume from adolescence, fumbling and fearful, to slightly less naive manhood. "Nightpiece with Figures," the story immediately preceding "September Dawn," ends with three boys in a darkened barn, silent after an elusive young nun's soft Gaelic farewell:

> with their happiness is mixed a melancholy as strange and perturbing, as though life itself and all the modes of life were inadequate. It is not a bitter melancholy like the melancholy of defeat, and in the morning, when they take to the country roads again, it will have passed. [71–72]

The memory of the young nun lingers with the boys; it also lingers into the next story.

The young Irish–speaking girl of "September Dawn" is no less mysterious to the romantic young warriors:

> Her appearance had a peculiar distinction that was almost beauty. Very straight and slender she was with a broad face that tapered to a point at the chin, a curious unsmiling mouth, large, sensitive nostrils, and wide-set, melancholy eyes. [87]

For those in a dishevelled flying column love is only a fleeting chance. After disbanding their column, because they "want to live for Ireland, not die for it" (75)—and sticking together they would all die—Hickey and Keown beat a haphazard retreat from Mallow toward the safety of the mountains of West Cork. Their frantic journey is devoid of glory or romance. They snatch bits of food on the run, not daring to stop. At nightfall they are in the vicinity of Hickey's aunt and make for the cottage. A girl is there, helping the old lady with the housework. To frightened, lonely young patriots on the run even a momentary romance would suffice to fill the emptiness.

As in most of the stories in *Guests of the Nation* the setting appears as natural and unobtrusive. From the flat, densely populated area around Mallow the two boys flee the encir-

cling ring of enemy troops, almost like animals, instinctively
toward the safety of the wilds. But place is never the primary
dimension in an O'Connor story. Some of the stories in the
volume take place in or near Cork City with its wet streets,
quays, steep hills, pubs, churches, lanes, and shops. Most of
the actual fighting stories are set in the countryside outside
Cork, in the rugged mountains around Macroom or the
gentle hills around Mallow. Setting for O'Connor emerges as
a complement to the voice of the story; setting is atmosphere.
Most of the stories are wrapped in darkness, casting the
disarray and desolation in silhouetted relief. Even time is
vague, for the historical moment dominates natural time.

"It was late September of the finest autumn that had been
known for years" (73). The story opens with that blunt
statement. The retreat of Hickey and Keown is made even
more treacherous by the oblique brilliance of the autumn sun
and the yellowing leaves. In this last gasp of summer the
"shafts of sunlight" (77) cast exaggerated shadows. Not the
normal desultory mist of the Irish countryside, the night is
remote and shadowy. The winds of the equinox which blow
so steadily in the south of Ireland shake loose the leaves and
keep the two tired lads edgy throughout the night. In this
autumnal transition they are suspended between fear and
melancholy. Hickey, sleepless and thoughtful, realizes "that
his life was a melancholy, aimless life, and that all this endless
struggle and concealment was but so much out of an existence
that would mean little anyhow" (92). He thinks of the girl in
the big house to whom he wanted to wave but didn't out of
the fear of discovery. That "desire for some human contact"
now returns "with all the dark power of nocturnal melancholy surging up beneath it; the feeling of his own loneliness,
his own unimportance, his own folly" (93). The swirling
wind wakes Keown who imagines in hysterical terror that
their pursuers have come. Only Hickey's fist silences his
snivelling. The point is that the swirling politics of violence
intrude even into this serene and natural setting.

In the gathering half-light before dawn Hickey smokes a cigarette and watches at the window. As the grey fog hugging the yard below lifts, "minute by minute," Hickey perceives

> all about him broken slates, with straw and withered leaves that rustled when the wind blew them about. The mist cleared farther, and he saw the trees looking much barer than they had looked the day before, with broken branches and the new day showing in great, rugged patches between them. . . . Light, a cold, wintry, forbidding light suffused the chill air. The birds were singing. [97]

The natural passage from verdant summer to desolate winter occurs as a shadow line as indecipherable as the dawn. Below in the kitchen Hickey finds Sheela returning with a bucket of turf. "They scarcely spoke" (98). In the light of the "newborn flame" he kisses her and

> for him in that melancholy kiss an ache of longing was kindled, and he buried his face in the warm flesh of her throat as the kitchen filled with the acrid smell of turf; while the blue smoke drifting through the narrow doorway was caught and whirled headlong through grey fields and dark masses of trees upon which an autumn sun was rising. [98]

Grotesques and silhouettes caught in the death-dealing hysteria of war find a hope as barren as the autumn dawn, a life-affirming melancholy that pervades the entire volume. The encroaching chill and darkness of winter signal an end of summer, but in the fleeting human contact lies a minimal hope for a new beginning.

As the emotional center of the volume "September Dawn" mediates the numbed thoughtfulness of the first and last stories with the thoughtless frenzy of the intervening stories. Its betweenness is the emotional condition of passage, and in the poignant layering of national transition and personal growth lies the lonely voice. The volume begins in war and ends in a temporal vacuum resembling peace. The man in "After Fourteen Years" could be visiting Bantry at almost any historical moment, for history pales in the face of personal considerations. He could just as well be going back after forty years, because life for him has settled into polite encrustation; it is settled and there is nothing to hope for. The same can be said for Henry Conran whose death was reported prematurely, and yet perhaps not, for he seems more dead than alive anyway. Death weighs heavily on "The Sisters" as well, a story about two sisters living alone, one of whom cares for the other and then dies suddenly leaving the "mad" sister on her own. These three stories about the process of aging and natural death fit the prevailing silhouette of death in the preceding war stories. Whereas the war stories concern the particular change from adolescence to maturity, these stories deal with the general reality of passing from one condition in life to another. But they share with the entire volume a sense of return, a backward look at once melancholy and hopeful.

The final story of the volume returns to the crisis of adolescence. "The Procession of Life" ties together much of the volume, both in tone and theme. The voice is a male voice looking back on the confusion and anxiety of growing up. What encloses the young hero of the story is his provincial Cork environment in general, his brutal father in particular. Larry's beloved mother has been dead almost a year; his obstinate father, on the night in question, has locked him out of the house. (O'Connor at the same age found himself locked out almost every time he went to the Gaelic League Hall with Corkery.) Alternately elated and miserable, he wanders along the quays, which are "lonely and full of shadows" (264), until he finds a watchman's sentry box. "The river made a clucking, lonely sound against the quay wall" (264). Larry is adrift and lonely, seeking some measure of human contact, but the grizzled old watchman chases him away when a lady of the night appears. The scene is a portrait of loneliness: three of the loneliest creatures imaginable huddled at one of those places of futility which one still finds on just about any public works site in Ireland. To Larry the

woman seems a "magical creature" (269). Her perfume he
finds "overpowering and sweet" (270). At the same time the
watchman falls under her spell. The old and the young, the
bitter and the naive share a radical lonesomeness. The woman's touch sends "a shiver of pleasure through him" (271)
and the watchman's competitive reproof cowers him. A con-
stable resolves the stand-off by sending the woman away to
meet him later. Whiskey and cigarettes warm three men of the
night. At the end of the story Larry disobeys the policeman's
order to stay with the old man and returns home jaunty and
confident and ready to defy his surly father. It is another
"playboy of the western world" perhaps; generation after
generation echoing the same lonely voice, adolescence,
maturity, and old age improvising solace in the face of cold
separation.

Seeking to capture in his own volume of stories something
of the unity of Turgenev, Moore, and Joyce, O'Connor gave
special force to the stories that open and close *Guests of the
Nation*. The lonely voice of "The Procession of Life" circles
the entire volume, signaling the passage from hysterical romance to melancholy realism. It stands somewhat apart from
the rest of the volume in terms of treatment, yet complements
the overall ambiance. Curiously, it represents the kind of
story for which O'Connor later became famous, the Larry
Delaney story of childhood and adolescence. The voice is
lyrical but not altogether personal; although there are distinct
autobiographical overtones, O'Connor's natural reserve dis-
courages too facile identification. Loneliness is embodied
rather than indulged, and in the detached, backward look
characteristic of nearly every story in the volume, the voices
generate a life of their own.

Likewise, the title story that opens the volume stands apart.
There is nothing else quite like it in O'Connor's work; its
brilliance and integrity are beyond question. In "Guests of
the Nation" O'Connor backs away from chauvinism and
hysteria far enough to allow a glimpse of the characters' tragic

impotence, but not so far as to miss their emotional vibra-
tions. Thrown together by the vagaries of war, three Irish
rebels and their two English hostages come to personal terms
over cards and share a momentary truce in conversation. But
national priorities take precedence over individual loyalties;
abstract retribution undermines concrete friendship. After
"assassinating" the two helpless hostages the hero-narrator
finds himself in a melancholy vacuum: "It is so strange what
you feel at such moments, and not to be written after-
wards. . . . I was somehow very small and very lonely. And
anything that ever happened to me after I never felt the same
about again" (19).

O'Connor has not indicted the rebels nor their cause;
neither has he vindicated violence. Rather he has isolated its
horrible effects at the moment of impact. For him human
dignity and rationality inevitably yield to the sudden impulse,
to the unpredictable and passing moment. So although there
is nothing quite like it in the rest of O'Connor's writing,
"Guests of the Nation" contains these qualities which are
unmistakably O'Connor's—it is simple, it possesses tight
narrative design and lively drama, and it carries sparse revela-
tions in language direct and alive. Most of all, the story
embodies that "lyric cry in the face of destiny."

Like most of his stories, "Guests of the Nation" came from
someone else, though O'Connor stamped it with his own
particular sympathies. As nearly as I can tell he heard the
essential germ of the story about the killing of two English
soldiers in reprisal for the killing of some Irish rebels from
someone in the Gormanstown Internment Camp. Apparently, there had been circulating in Kerry a rumored tale
about two English defectors who had been working on farms
for some time before a zealous rebel leader, perhaps even
O'Donovan Rossa, took them as spies and ordered their
execution. A variation on the anecdote had it that the two
were to be murdered in the milking shed of an isolated Kerry
farm. When the simple farmer objected to disallowing the

men benefit of clergy, his strong-willed wife thrust him aside, took the gun and shot the two Englishmen herself. In the internment camp O'Connor read the prison journals of John Mitchell and Michael Davitt and heard about the exploits of O'Donovan Rossa. It is probably not coincidental, therefore, that the dogmatic rebel commander, Jeremiah Donovan, resembles that early Fenian hero, Jeremiah O'Donovan Rossa, friend of Mitchell, O'Leary, and Davitt.

No matter where O'Connor got his story and no matter how obliquely he grafted it onto different characters and situations, "Guests of the Nation" emerged in the telling as a tightly designed and provocative story. It has become a classic story, honored by many imitations including Brendan Behan's "The Hostage." In "Guests of the Nation" as in few of his other earlier stories, O'Connor rises above mere contrivance and literary fumbling to voice the sort of primary affirmation which he himself insisted was vital to great literature.

O'Connor finished writing "Guests of the Nation" late in March, 1930. He later felt that writing it had been something of a breakthrough. After all, he hadn't the slightest idea how to write stories. He certainly knew nothing about the sort of facts with which most other storytellers seemed to salt their prose. Quite by accident he discovered himself laughing and crying as he wrote "Guests of the Nation." He knew he had written a good story but for the life of him he couldn't tell why. The demise of AE's *Irish Statesman*, he wrote to Nancy McCarthy on April 3, 1930, had forced him to seek outlets in America, which he added "may be a blessing for me, really, though I shall have to bottle up my rage against the Gaels." At the same time he observed that "John Hendrick would smile at my all–too–careful preparations, my violence of self–criticism, but never mind, I shall write so that every word will have a meaning. . . ." Whatever it was, rage against Corkery's national consciousness or against his own fumbling prose, something was bottled up in O'Connor which made him quarrelsome at the library and moody at his flat. His stomach alternated between bad and worse. Exiled in Dublin, writing out the demons of his war experiences, and trying to convince Nancy to marry him, he must have felt the loneliest creature on God's earth.

II

Thus, when he received a telegram from *The Atlantic Monthly* accepting "Guests of the Nation," his exuberance was volcanic. He grabbed his amazed landlady, twirled her rejoicing around the kitchen, kissed her smartly, and rushed off to tell the news to Dermot. That morning the library was a noisy shambles until the two decided to take their celebration to Glendalough. Off they went for a great weekend of careless abandon; after all, the American magazine was paying O'Connor £150 for the story. What they forgot was that the money came later. Dermot chuckled all the way back to Dublin, while O'Connor drank and waited in the Glendalough Hotel until Dermot could return with enough money to cover their lavish celebration.

However, the enthusiasm with which that story was received by the editors of *The Atlantic Monthly* unfortunately failed to emerge in Britain, where O'Connor was trying to find a publisher for the entire volume. He was encouraged by various literary friends to send his set of stories to Edward Garnett, the noted English critic who had already "discovered" Liam O'Flaherty and who would shortly do the same for Sean O'Faolain. Garnett's judgment apparently ranked somewhere near gospel in the minds of British publishers, so it seemed fatal when Garnett returned the stories with the acrid comment that O'Connor had no power of observation. What was more, he recommended O'Connor read O'Flaherty. O'Connor was dismayed more than crushed. Certainly Garnett could be no more critical of his writing than he was himself. In September, still waiting to hear from Macmillan, he wrote to Nancy:

> As for the book I really am not in the least worried, call me liar as often as you please. I am exalted when I am writing a good story; when it is written I have little or no interest in it, except to revise; and then only when the old glory flashes over it again for an instant. I am thrilled if it please someone; if it does not please I don't care.

Perhaps the insouciance was a trifle posed, but apparently O'Connor was less bothered by the Garnett snub than AE, Nancy, and Sean Hendrick. He was too busy trying to bring his novel, *The Saint and Mary Kate,* into shape and too worried about his health.

With the anticipated publication of *Guests of the Nation,* Frank O'Connor the author was on his way. His real–life counterpart Michael O'Donovan, however, was still somewhat adrift. His "infertile in–between periods" of loneliness and boredom were exaggerated by Nancy McCarthy's staunch refusal to marry him and by his chronic stomach problem. For weeks on end that winter he lived on little but baby food. Whether from his long hours of work or from his shyness, O'Connor had still managed to make few friends in Dublin. Rainy days, bad plays, dull conversations, and endless cigarettes only served to magnify his desperate need for human contact.

During the winter of 1930–31 O'Connor was almost continually sick, either with gastritis or with painful neck boils. His friend and physician, Dr. Richard Hayes, believed he had a gangrenous abscess and that the boils on his neck were but the external evidence. Furthermore, the Greater Dublin Act made it apparent that Dermot would soon be forced to take another post, leaving O'Connor with only a shadow of his library. That meant he would have no one to walk the streets of Ballsbridge with, no one to listen to the gramophone with,

no one to commiserate about his chaotic lovelife with. He had
written war out of his system but not women.

It is said that Turgenev once told Tolstoy that he could not
write unless he was in love. Frank O'Connor probably would
have said it that directly, but it is obvious that his greatest
productivity came when he was romantically involved with a
woman. By the same token, his times of dearth as a writer
occurred when he felt a vacuum of love or when he was
caught in tangled relationships that blurred the mystique of
love for him. His strong and stormy friendships with men
were collaborations in shared enthusiasms; his relationships
with women were romantic pursuits of magic on one hand
and stability on the other. He saw love through a veil of
literature and idealized women from afar.

Actually, in the company of women O'Connor was so
sensitive, as one woman put it, that he never seemed "to
know whether he [was] standing on his head or his feet."[6]
Once he surprised Dermot Foley by agreeing to attend a
meeting of a notoriously "precious" literary group, then
surprised him "still more by turning into a pub and swallow-
ing a double whiskey, since he seldom drank at that time."[7]
What Dermot didn't know was that O'Connor always took a
drink or two whenever visiting strangers, to brace himself for
the ordeal. Not that it helped much, for he "had only to enter
a strange house or talk to a stranger to make a complete fool"
of himself. After a particularly embarrassing evening at the
Francis Hacketts's, Joseph O'Neill tried to defend O'Connor's penetrating mind to an offended "lady," only to con-
clude that "O'Connor never does himself justice except when
he sits down alone to write."[8]

In society, O'Connor was ill at ease, awkward, and naive.
From shyness he talked too much and regretted most of it
afterwards. One never knew whether he would be contentious, giddy, churlish, or totally silent, masks he wore which
allowed few people to get at first impression any sense of his
genuine warmth and depth. But alone, reading or writing, he

was totally at ease and marvellously controlled. It was evidence again of that double life he had been leading since childhood, one in the real world of "drudgery and limitation," of grammar and manners, and one in his imaginary world of chivalric daydreams and foreign languages, music and poetry.

One of the weaknesses of a mother's boy is a lifelong need of female presence. O'Connor was helpless domestically, unable to perform even the simplest chores like making breakfast, choosing a suitable lamp, or hanging a picture to the wall. He confessed to being "hagridden" without a woman to look after him. One of the basic reasons for his chronic stomach problem was his atrocious eating habits—his "rut of occasional meals and general abstraction." "Whether or not there is a woman looking after me," he wrote to Nancy late in 1930, "can usually be observed by noting whether or not there is a large stain of cigarette ash on the front of my pants." O'Connor was hopeless emotionally without a woman. He hated to be alone, yet needed solitude for writing. He was desperate for the magic and inspiration of a loving relationship, yet equally insistent on time and space for dreaming. Throughout his life he sought the constant, enduring, and silent presence of the sort his mother gave him.

Shortly after O'Connor moved from Castleville to Molly Alexander's house in Ranelagh, his mother came to Dublin for the first of a string of lengthy visits. From then on she came to Dublin almost every spring and fall. She always spent part of his holidays in Glengarriff with him. Of course, he came home for Christmas. They needed each other, the spoiled poor boy and the aging orphan–mother. From the very first Minnie got on well with Molly, who attended to her son and loved him from afar. Minnie spent her time tidying his digs and writing letters back to her husband in Cork. She worried about the drink so she also wrote to her friends in the square; nothing could cure her of the belief that Big Mick needed her mothering attention too. During the day she shopped with Molly in the village or went by herself into town. In the evening she and O'Connor and Molly enjoyed extended tea and conversation. O'Connor was homesick in Dublin and within a few days so was she. So they talked mainly about Cork or rather she regaled him with anecdotes about the place. After tea they generally walked; O'Connor listened as Minnie made Ranelagh and Ballsbridge and Donny-brook hospitable, which is to say she made them seem like Cork. She always retired early as much for O'Connor as for herself. Though nearly seventy she was still energetic; she was also perceptive enough to know that her son the writer would be needing to write.

Her visits proved to be about the only time O'Connor was not susceptible to his Byronic melancholy. She was the ointment for everything. In October 1930, after he had moved from Chelmsford to Angelsea Road, Minnie came for her longest visit. She found him almost comfortable; Molly had dressed up his new digs with curtains and other feminine touches. She also found him ill and irritable. For months he had been avoiding the theatre and all other public events. *Guests of the Nation* had sapped his spirit completely. By the time his mother left in December he had recovered enough from the gastritis and from the string of exasperations to take up work on his novel again.

Before moving to Dublin, O'Connor's romantic involve-ment with young women had been remarkably tame; he talked a more up-to-date sexual ethic than he practiced. In Cork, besides that decorous courtship with Nancy McCar-thy, he had been "pals" with the O'Leary girls and had entertained fantasies about Natalie Murphy. In Dublin his female pals included Mary Manning, Anne Crowley, and Irene Haugh; his imagined affairs were countless. For some reason he felt constrained to inform Nancy of the new women in his life, always the same gallant, bouncy, sassy sort of girl. Not long after coming to Dublin he fell hopelessly in love with Meriel Moore, an actress at the Gate. He even went so far as to land a part in a silly comedy in which she played the female lead just to be near her. Later it was Ruth Draper, a friend of Francis Hackett, who owned a motor car and took him on gay rides to Wicklow. Then too, there was Ethel Montgomery, a woman twice his age whom he met at AE's. "That's the sort of woman I'd like to marry—if ever," he told Dermot one Sunday evening after she had interrupted the burly old saint's monologue with an outburst of laughter. The more irrepressible a woman's gaiety and the more spontaneously erupting her wit, the more she seemed to represent his ideal of womanhood, his mother.

Molly Alexander, his young landlady, had been placed in a vulnerable position by her husband's frequent absences from the home. She decided to take in a lodger as much for the security of a man in the house as for the additional income. Because he was wrapped up in his long-distance romance with Nancy and because Molly was married, nothing romantic ever developed between them. Still, they managed to share one of the closest friendships O'Connor was ever to enjoy with a woman his own age. She woke him every morning, served him breakfast in the tiny kitchen at the back of the house, and tidied his room during the day. Often they would sit and talk after tea. But usually O'Connor would eat and retire to his room to write. It was here that he wrote the stories of *Guests of the Nation*.

Molly Alexander was one of those simple, unpretentious people toward whom, Dermot asserts, O'Connor was "warmth itself." With her there was none of his cast-iron arrogance. To her he was a simple man, easy to talk to. Any man who loved his mother as much as O'Connor, couldn't be all bad, she thought. She admired his diligence in writing every evening after working a full day in the library. Occasionally, she would read whatever pages were in his typewriter. Once she even asked him about what he was writing and whether he would ever read something of it to her. Sheepishly at first, leafing his fingers through his hair, and then with great pomp he read his latest story. One story in particular, "The Sisters," pleased her because he had taken it from an incident she had related to him one evening. (O'Connor took stories from anyone—postman, plumber, or landlady.)

The nearly two years there at Chelmsford Road had been good years. It was in Molly's sitting room downstairs that he and Dermot spent hours listening to music on his prized gramophone. Usually it was Mozart or Beethoven, but occasionally Dermot could convince him to tolerate Schubert or Bach. One evening, in a particularly mischievous mood, O'Connor produced a new acquisition which he claimed to be Mozart. Dermot squirmed patiently until O'Connor rose to turn the disk. "Who the bloody hell is that really?" Dermot roared. "It can't be Mozart." O'Connor, with an unnoticed twinkle in his eye, simply replaced the needle and sat down again to listen to the other side. When it was over Dermot, who deferred to him in almost everything except library mechanics, broke the silence first. "Well, if that's Mozart, then I'm Brahms." "How did you know?" O'Connor replied. "Know what?" "That was actually Brahms," O'Connor confessed gleefully. "Blackguard," Dermot shouted over his booming laughter. "I'll never trust you again." "Sir," said O'Connor, "and I shall never question your taste in music again." Their laughter woke one of Molly's children.

Only on the rare occasion did O'Connor entertain a woman at Chelmsford Road. One evening Mary Manning decided that he needed to improve his social graces. So, with a bundle of moderately decorous yet danceable gramophone records she came one evening to teach him how to dance. For something over an hour she counted steps and cursed his unruly feet. O'Connor gave it an earnest try but with every awkward stumble he grew more frustrated. By the time Dermot arrived, after closing the library at nine o'clock, O'Connor was in a right pique. Dermot, on hearing the strangely unMozartian sounds, was more than a trifle curious. When he entered O'Connor announced in triumph that he was learning to dance and would Dermot just watch this. After three or four grimaces from Mary Manning, Dermot was finding it hard to contain the laughter. "And I suppose you can do better?" his sweaty boss challenged. Of course he hardly cared that indeed Dermot could do better. At least if Dermot were dancing, then he would be spared the indignity of this athletic nonsense. Following two cigarettes and a few dances by Dermot and Mary, they all three enjoyed another good chuckle. The children didn't awaken, but Molly was more than a little perturbed.

Shortly after publishing *Guests of the Nation,* O'Connor moved from Molly's house. He had grown restless and irritable. It is true that he wanted a place with his own furniture, but it is probably just as true that he had grown uneasy with Molly's attention to him. Moreover, just about everyone who made Dublin liveable for him was disappearing—Dermot to Ennis, Norah and Geoffrey Phibbs to London. Nancy was as obdurate as ever. Besides, the library was now only a job and his stomach was in outright rebellion. Finally, he had not yet been able to get a fix on his novel. But mainly, I suspect, it was Molly. Like so many of the women in his life she had been drawn as much by his practical helplessness as by his creativity and magnetic personality. She had loved him and mothered him. In any case, beginning a lifelong pattern of parting, he left. Displaced and unsure of himself, he thus began a pattern that continued throughout the 1930s of one move after the other.

III

In April of 1931 O'Connor mentioned by way of an aside in a letter to Nancy that his novel was about half finished. Though he had no way of knowing it, his relationship with her was also about half finished. Already, there had been three years of frustratingly proper courtship, most of it

carried on through the post. Yet to come were three more
years of self-imposed torture. It was her chastity and piety
against his audacity and impiety. But she was safe and she was
above all from Cork. And O'Connor still needed an anchor
of sorts. By his own admission to her this was not really a
love affair:

> and because of that I think all the more of that queer little lane off
> Winter's Hill, and that night or rather that morning after The
> Round Table; the little window all lit up and·the people who said
> the rosary inside; I think of it as if it were something out of a
> book that I had read long ago and of which I could remember
> nothing else, not even its author nor its name.

Something out of a book indeed, for love was part of that
entire mystique of romantic moods and romantic words. As
he was in love with writing, so O'Connor was at this time in
love with love, trapped in a sense by its mystique.

Oh, not that he did not know—he knew rationally. Actually, he was so absorbed in the loneliness and worry of his
writing that this need for love blurred his mind. For instance,
in one winter letter he opens with this paragraph:

> What a mean creature you are! And how weak I am! For just as
> I had made up my mind never to write to you again I began
> reconstructing the Castleblayney story (which may yet prove a
> masterpiece) and fell again hopelessly in love with the typescript
> Nance that the very real coldblooded inconsiderate Nance was
> dissolved in a romantic shower of gold.

At times, however, he could cut through that self-absorption
and be compassion itself, particularly at moments of crisis for
Nancy (only crisis that had nothing to do with himself).
When her friend Gracie O'Shea died in July, 1929, he wrote
two very supportive and tender letters. Toward the end of the
first, after observing how suffering acts as a merciful opiate on
itself, he concludes:

It is very rough on you now, but you will be all right. You have what I have not got and what I grudge you whole heartedly, tremendous resilience. . . .

It will all pass—quicker than you know. But while you can grieve, do. It is one of the few things worth while and perhaps the purest thing in our lives. I wish I could be more helpful, but you know me for what I am, a dour doleful heathen who contemplates the universe with a scowl and sees in everything a snare.

Actually, he exaggerated her resiliency, which was merely a fatalistic assessment of her abilities and a resigned acceptance of life's limited hopes.

O'Connor believed that what he needed was a strong woman, "not a knock-kneed hypercritical hypersensitive pathological case like myself." In a gesture of self-dramatization he ended another letter by exclaiming: "Russell is right about me; I am a romantic and the realism is only a kink. Realism be damned! It's only a sort of spiritual cold storage." Nancy was realist enough to know that marriage with O'Connor would not work; she had simply adjusted to it. O'Connor probably knew it but persisted in bucking the tide. Loving a woman, distant and unattainable, was the chivalric way, the "literary" way. Frustration was the price one paid for Romance.

Since he saw life through a "veil of literature" even his lovers became part of the texture of his literary life. His letters to Nancy resembled those of Chekhov to Olga, which in fact he once instructed Nancy to read. As such they represent self-defence. O'Connor was testing the limits of his artistic vision against a congenial intelligence. His tone was usually confessional. He shared with her the travail of writing, his moods of anguish, the self-doubt, and occasionally even his tentative delight in his abilities. After all, she had been supplying him with story material so her opinions were hardly those of an outsider. Yet he complained again and again of her superficial gossip when what he needed was a good story. He also needed objective details about Cork for his novel. She enthusiastically assisted him during the spring of 1931 by taking countless photographs around Cork. In a small way then, Nancy was as much a collaborator in his early writing efforts as a sounding board for his highly volatile opinions and for his stifling depressions. She believed in him, probably more than he did himself, and encouraged him constantly. Her resistence to his pressure to live with him was due less to moral scruples than to a deeper concern that she would hinder him from writing the masterpieces she knew he had in him.

The novel, begun in October, 1930, and half finished in April, 1931, was nearing completion in June. O'Connor had detached himself almost completely from his little library in Pembroke since the Greater Dublin Act, even going so far as to write in his office during the day.[9] Not knowing how to love, he groped for something resembling affection with Nancy. And not knowing how to write, he fumbled for style. AE spent hours with him pouring over his novel, struggling with him "for mastery of the theme." All O'Connor could say was that it was his religious novel. AE considered it a philosophical mouthpiece. On June 14 O'Connor wrote to Nancy:

> I don't like to speak too much of the novel at this closing stage (scowls at typewriter and attempts to readjust the ribbon) but it may be a masterpiece. Anyway in spots it is long miles ahead of what I have done before and it is simply burning its way about in my mind. I wish whether you go to Switzerland or England you would call here and read and discuss it before it is sent off. It must be finished for the end of July.

Then, flush with confidence, he retorts to her latest bubble-bursting criticism:

> (Irritably) Why of course, girl, I am a genius. Realize that when I left Cork two and a half years ago I was writing in prose nothing

but balderdash, that when I was here for six months I wrote After Forty Years and have progressed from that through September Dawn, through Guests to Conran and the Patriarch, and am now engaged in leaving these behind me at the rate of two hundred and twenty miles an hour. And all this in spite of physical ailments and a shyness of human beings such as no writer before me ever had.

Nancy sent the photos, of course, prompting O'Connor to admit that they helped to recall details which his memory had confused. "I shall never, never begin a novel again without going over my ground with a camera. The detail one gets wrong is not so important as the detail one misses."

By the end of June the old self-doubt had returned. "The book is a glugger," he wrote on a dismal Saturday morning. Thursday he had consoled himself that if not a masterpiece, it was at least a "readable bit of humorous writing." Then on Friday night even that hope had fled, thrusting him from an improvisational fury to disconsolate melancholy.

The truth is that I know nothing whatever of novel writing or didn't while I was writing it. A novel—I define for your benefit—is the smallest number of characters in the least number of situations necessary to precipitate a given crisis. But what use are definitions when my book is the greatest number of characters in the greatest number of situations leading up to a non-existent crisis? It's deplorable. A man with half my talent would have done it ten times better. I have Mozart's fatal gift of melody only my melodies are characters; characters for which a real novelist would have given his soul spring up at every page and I enjoy myself, and then—no more.

Dermot Foley, who had not yet departed for Ennis, laughingly chided saying that this was merely the opinion of the weekend. By Monday when he finally posted the letter O'Connor could scribble at the bottom of the last page his fervent thanks to St. Anthony for having rediscovered the subject of the book.

So his emotions continued to roller coaster. Three days later he wrote again to Nancy:

> How great and rich the times are now. Wednesday a visit from Norah McGuinness, Thursday a gathering peace about my book, Friday a letter from A.E. (consoling me) and tonight a letter from you (consoling me). . . . Not that I have reached anything like my old exultation, but reading certain bits I was profoundly moved by a sort of physical tenderness which I know is in myself though it is in nothing I have written up to this; and I understand why it is that for months I have felt a curious passion for birds and dogs and children, because ultimately we become what we write even if the change is not perceptible to others.

The rest of the letter is playful. He chides her for misreading Lawrence whose stories he finds the only real English stories worth reading. Then he requests a snapshot of Nancy in her bathing attire. "You never know what it will inspire," he quips. Finally, in a scribbled postscript he lets her know that he has settled on a title for his novel; it is to be called *The Saint and Mary Kate*.

Meanwhile, he had received proofs of *Guests of the Nation* and sent them to Nancy cautioning her not to show them to anyone. He found it amusing that Macmillan editors had recommended reconsideration of "all Anglo-Saxon words beginning with 'b'," suggesting "jade" instead. He also expressed slight dissatisfaction with their exaggerated enthusiasm about the title story. When the volume finally appeared in September he was still chuckling and still slightly irritated. Reviewers paid little attention to his own personal favorites. And comparing him to Turgenev seemed somewhat out of proportion, if not downright blasphemy. About all the lavish praise for his promise as a writer he simply scribbled on the copy of the Macmillan announcement he sent to Nancy—"We Shall See!" At the end of the letter in which the announcement and a few clippings were enclosed, he admits that it is a "disgruntled egotistical letter," but still "one publishes a first book but once, and whether one lives or dies the bloom will soon be off the rose."

More than anything else what disturbed O'Connor was not hearing from Corkery to whom he had sent a special signed copy. "Catch me do it again." His first book, his biggest step into the world of writing, and no acknowledgement from the man who had actually got him started. Not much actually from anyone in his home town. "Oh, Cork! Cork!" he moaned to Nancy. And what would they ever think of the novel just around the corner.

The flurry of that novel behind him, his annual holiday with his mother having degenerated into a feud with his father, O'Connor was again caught in one of his Byronic depressions. Exhaustion and poor eating habits caused his stomach problems to flare up again. The Angelsea lodgings where he had written *The Saint and Mary Kate* now felt confining and inhospitable, the library even less congenial. So, in the fall, feeling displaced and restless, he decided to move once again. In December with an acquaintance named Paddy Corr he took a flat in a huge house called "Trenton" just across from the Royal Dublin Society.

The novel was finished; all that remained, besides the proof stage, was the small matter of a dedication. O'Connor had never considered anyone except Nancy McCarthy, but when he mentioned it to her she refused flatly. Supposing her reticence had something to do with her job, he implored her to reconsider. What she could not tell him, or even admit to herself, was that she was in the throes of a nervous break-down herself. To her mind the *Saint* went mad at the end of the novel; worried about doing the same (a worry based largely on her mother's mental history) she did not need any additional impetus. Locked in his own "fit of gathering gloom," he had no way of comprehending her mind. Her refusal stung him deeply. He eventually dedicated the novel to his mother.

By the beginning of 1932 O'Connor was quite at sea about

his novel. Actually, he was at sea about nearly everything—suffering the agonies of gastritis and painful boils, drinking too much, and entertaining a "chorus girl." He wrote to Nancy that with all the pent-up hatred of his heart he hated the *Saint*. "Why didn't I stick to short stories which I know I can do on my head instead of mucking about with a form of which I know nothing and for which I care less?" Advance reviews were confusing him even more. The *Derry Journal* attacked his sneering attitude toward the church and accused him of writing on a dungheap, even going so far as to imply that he must be some sort of sex maniac. However, *The Observer* gave him excellent advance coverage. That response would be true his entire career—praise from England and America and condemnation from Ireland. The misplaced enthusiasm afforded *Guests of the Nation* had perplexed him, and he was sure that this novel "will annoy everybody except the artists so it will cancel out." This pattern too would persist throughout his life—writing for the common reader, he gathered more acclaim from the intelligensia. He was not prepared either for Nancy's annoyance. She was the common reader for whom the book was written and when she read the slip proofs late in January some of the language struck her as disgusting. Caught between hating and adoring her, O'Connor was shattered.

From the very beginning O'Connor had sought her opinions. She was his closest friend in Cork and this was a Cork novel. No one else understood the ambiguities he felt for his home. He confided to her not only a monetary motive in writing a novel—to make enough to be able to retire to Spain to write another—but a more delicate motive as well—to rival Daniel Corkery's *A Threshold of Quiet*. "At least the Saint is an artistic failure!" Some years later he drafted an essay on Corkery in which he contended that Martin Cloyne and Stevie Galvin represent the two suspended halves of Corkery's own character.[8] Into Cloyne, O'Connor wrote, Corkery put his real self, his fastidiousness, humour, and self-control, while in Stevie Galvin, who might be J. J. O'Connor, he drew his anti-self; a self he had uprooted, cast aside and yet thought of with longing and perhaps envy. Stevie is as unstable as Cloyne is self-controlled; a myriad-minded man, whose thought ranges to the Poles, who can't think of a boat without learning navigation and plotting the book he will write about his travels.

What O'Connor saw in *A Threshold of Quiet* was perhaps what he wrote into *The Saint and Mary Kate*—the pirate chief opposing the bespectacled scholar, natural instinct set against rational will, romanticism circling realism.

The Saint and Mary Kate was Frank O'Connor's religious love book, a testament to the magic of love and the exuberance of faith. The treatment was entirely from without because the drama was all too within that passionate variety show in his own mind. When Nancy observed that the characters seemed to her like museum pieces he agreed, though claiming the same could be said of a Dostoevsky novel or an Elizabethan play. "It's just a question of approach. Seen close enough anything appears monstrous while if one stands far enough away (Guests) the most monstrous thing appears natural." The more interior the crisis the more externalized the treatment. But what he observed later of Corkery's *A Threshold of Quiet* may be as true of his own novel, "a work of art in the Freudian sense of a spiritual conflict in the author's mind given external expression."

If *The Saint and Mary Kate* is the work of a young man groping for a suitable theme, it is also the work of an Irishman writing to locate a cohesive Irish consciousness. On one hand, then, the novel is a private quest and an act of love. As such it reveals something of the character of the man who wrote it. On the other hand, this novel is a public portrait and an act of defiance. To understand it is to catch a glimpse of the nature of his circumstances. For O'Connor to do battle with the provincial narrowness of Cork was to encounter his own provincialism; to answer Corkery was to confront his spiritual father. *Guests of the Nation* represents the work of the son fumbling for style; *The Saint and Mary Kate* is the work of the lover fumbling for substance. It is the natural extension of the life-affirming voice of "September Dawn" and "The Procession of Life."

O'Connor once said that Ireland always looks out on the world through windows and doors. Mary Kate McCormick and Phil Dinan peer from the dark, confining monotony of a Cork tenement called the "Dolls' House" toward the light and freedom of the outside world. Their "tragedy of innocence," as O'Connor himself termed it, resembles the double doors so prevalent up and down the untidy, noisy lanes of this unacknowledged Irishtown—half open and half shut, the brutality of circumstance blocking the delicacy of hope. O'Connor neither romanticizes poverty nor condemns wealth; the abstraction of social class dissolves before the richness of emotion and language within this Native Stream. Far enough away to appear natural, close enough to be monstrous—that is how you feel toward the desperate, volatile poverty of the Dolls' House, an eighteenth-century house once occupied by the rich and taken over since the Famine by the poor. A two-story tenement occupied now by six to eight families, the Dolls' House sits just off the North Mall near St. Vincent's by the quays. Just around the corner is Coal Quay, a teeming market where the shawlies barter for sparse goods and trade lavish insults.

Mary Kate, the illegitimate daughter of the tenement's "loose woman," is one of those people for whom even the Cork quays are "magical miles."[11] The beauty of the trees and the river and the surrounding hills stands in mocking contrast to the decay of the Dolls' House. But this is her school, and in it "she studied earnestly" (48), learning "that behind all the love of women for men lies a secret sorrow" (47). A woman who throws herself out of a window is picked up dead without word or tear. Crying children of a harlot mother gather around a sobbing neighbor woman and

wait for her drunken husband to return, to vomit, and to rush
at them with a razor, forcing them to take refuge in still
another room of the tenement, to sleep on still another floor.
One idol after another toppled for Mary Kate in this blighted
college of despair.

Not long before she turns fifteen she meets Phil Dinan,
who lives with his mother, a quiet, devout charwoman, at the
back of the tenement. Unlike Mary Kate he is a model of
piety and self control. He has "that complete disregard of
worldly appearance that belongs to a saint" (218). His mother
works six days a week so that he can keep to his books rather
than becoming a messenger boy. He is also obsessed by the
clock. Every morning, for instance, he and Mary Kate attend
Mass to pray for his dying mother. When Mary Kate over-
sleeps one morning, Phil refuses to call again unless she
attaches a note to her door explicitly stating her intention to
accompany him to Mass. He has even counted the steps
between the Dolls' House and the church. On the unlikely
affinity of these two "innocents" the novel turns; her magical
enthusiasm and the intensity of her longing for "something
else" swirling around his chastened severity and shy restraint.

The first half of the novel, set entirely in the Dolls' House,
presents the opposite responses of Phil and Mary Kate to their
blighted and restrictive surroundings. Each is dependent only
upon himself: she by her mother's way of life and he by his
mother's death. His studious piety drives him further into
himself and her sentimental fantasies always seem to leave her
with herself. She is frustrated, for example, by Phil's prudish
control. "It was a great curse, she thought, tossing restlessly
in her bed, to fall in love for the first time with a boy whose
tastes in women ran to motherhood, and who attached to
kissing an importance out of all proportion to the event"
(131). But both she and Phil are immensely lonely. One scene
in particular emphasizes their mutual need for each other.
Walking back from his mother's burial, Phil, accompanied by
Mary Kate, stops to buy a watch. Mary Kate is shocked by

the "brutal insensitiveness" (89) and selfishness of this act. Silently he buys one for himself and then one for her. The tenderness of the gesture stuns her momentarily. Then he adds that now she can be on time for Mass. O'Connor extracts every ounce of emotional drama from this almost wordless scene. It is a poignant moment in which two people try to offset the pain of death in equally valid and equally incomplete ways.

In the second half of the novel, Phil abandons his judgment and travels to Dublin to rescue Mary Kate who has gone to visit the man she supposes to be her father. The fight with McCormick and the strange events on the road back to Cork force Phil and Mary Kate together. Returning home for her is anguish; she has sought her past and found it empty. Phil, however, "was tasting in innocence the joy of discovery" (220), the discovery of a future. Of course, the past intrudes on him as well when his mother appears to him in an apparition. "A loneliness filled the room that did not come from the night outside, but from the night within himself, as though there were reaches of his nature that he had never known of or walked in" (237). In the end he retreats into the sanctity of his abstractions and the novel closes on a note of unresolved separation.

While writing *Guests of the Nation*, O'Connor had sketched out a story in his journal about a character modeled after a fellow lodger whose compulsive attention to detail, whether counting the number of steps between Castleville and the nearest chapel or collecting overdue debts from friends, seemed almost saintly to an undisciplined, impetuous librarian. He intended to use this "boy's religious phase" to externalize his own struggle to bring his own chaotic life into some sort of rational order. Indeed, Phil's "fidgets" resemble the compulsive efficiency of O'Connor's fellow lodger as his bookish seriousness mirrors something of O'Connor's own character. The problem was that the Saint reflected nothing of that adventuresome dreamer of Harrington Square who survived the squalor of his surroundings by the intensity of his dreams.

Realizing with AE's help that his theme was still the crisis of growing up in Cork, O'Connor dredged up two stories written three or four years earlier. "The Ring" (*Irish States-man*, 28 July 1928) is an almost Chekhovian account of a tale told by a woman, an orphan girl faintly resembling O'Connor's mother, who settled for the one who asked her only to find herself cast on the street by the drunken brute. In "The Awakening" (*Dublin Magazine*, July 1928) another young girl—equally daring, gay, and carefree—comes to life and leaves her empty home and saintly boyfriend who is serious, shy, and responsible. The women of these two stories draw heavily on the inspiration of the two women closest to O'Connor, his mother and Nancy McCarthy—the outcast and the romantic. Both ask more of life than their impoverished circumstances can deliver; they ask more than their men deliver too. So O'Connor's Hamlet, as he wrote to Nancy, was not the saintly boy but the spontaneous girl. O'Connor had often heard about the daughter of a prostitute who lived in his square, a girl who went off in search of her father and never returned. He found himself as captivated by his heroine as AE who speculated about what she would be like to live with.

O'Connor was in love when he wrote "The Awakening," whose heroine is the first fictional appearance of the O'Connor Woman—unpredictable, bright–eyed, witty, and a creature of instinct rather than intellect. It was a boy's image of girls, full of worship and dismay. Many of the girls in *Guests of the Nation* display that same carefree insolence—Norah in "Jo," Helen in "Soirée chez une Belle Jeune Fille," and the nun in "Nightpiece With Figures." They are all a bit like Ita O'Leary, Natalie Murphy, and Eileen Gould (O'Faolain)—all unorthodox girls from lively, secure homes unlike O'Connor's with its melancholy atmosphere. He held a curiously similar image of his mother and of Nancy. By the time he wrote *The Saint and Mary Kate* O'Connor was still in love, though no nearer marriage, in love with an image more fanciful than real of the quicksilver girl confronting the desolation around her with an amusing irrelevancy and a laughing eye.

As compelling and sensitive as it is in parts, *The Saint and Mary Kate* is not a successful novel. For one thing O'Connor took an abstraction too seriously and let it dictate his plot. For a novelist, even one given to thematic concerns, such an approach often signals a weakness; for a storyteller like O'Connor it is disastrous. The particular abstraction here is the opposition between two conflicting ways of life, represented by Mary Kate and Phil. For example, consider the poignant scene in which the two travellers share their feelings about love while huddling together inside a ruined cabin.

> 'Everybody,' said Eternal Boy as though he had not heard her, and quite unaware of that wan little smile Eternal Woman gave him in the darkness, 'has some passion that eats him up, and his will power is the only weapon he have against it. I haven't a strong will power, and I never had, but bad as it is it's all that stands between me and a shocking life.' [194]

Mary Kate, who has not only just kissed Phil but has confessed to being in love with her supposed father, doubts that her saintly companion has any passion at all. Phil, "his overburdened conscience staggering like an old ass mounting a hill" (193), admits that " 'tis lust" (195). Mary Kate's suppressed chuckle, forcing its way through her grief, is telling. The difference is that Mary Kate, "a poet though she did not write" (141), is groping instinctively for her past by this misadventure to Dublin. Phil, by contrast, has been ruthlessly carving out his future. Their emotional lives change in opposite directions on the road back to Cork—Mary Kate's from the magic of her dreams to the melancholy of regret, Phil's from restraint to panic. The future collides with her past, the past with his future. O'Connor's own pirate

chief and bespectacled scholar, those two sides of his character constantly at war, switch coats as it were, suspending the
moment in the loneliness of unbelonging.

   The dislocation of these two youngsters in time and space
stems from the tragic gap between dreams and realities,
between emotions and thoughts. A profound theme, to be
sure, and one that O'Connor would elucidate in more subtle
ways in later stories, but profound or not, a theme imposed on
situation and character calls attention to itself instead of
emerging naturally from the whole. O'Connor began by
writing about the Saint but soon let it become Mary Kate's
book, realizing perhaps that AE was right about his realism
merely being a kink. O'Connor became Mary Kate simply by
following his instinctive enthusiasms. Unfortunately, it was
not long before he turned, for various reasons, back to the
cold storage of his judgment.

   On the other hand, to his credit perhaps, O'Connor's
inclinations as a storyteller get in the way of his novel. He is
too easily diverted from his deterministic "tragedy of innocence." By his own critical standards, a novel requires a
society, not just a vague backdrop. O'Connor appears so
intrigued by the people that he barely elaborates on the world
in which they live, the world that supposedly crushes their
dreams. Still, the setting of the novel is drawn with such swift
sympathy that it strikes the reader as absolutely genuine, a
tribute Sean O'Faolain believed, "the only real tribute"
Cork's poor ever received. It is precisely his sympathy that
diverts O'Connor's attention. When he sketches a tenement
feud, or the face of one of Cork's "characters," or the tone of
an overheard conversation, he appears diverted by the potential story; a passing glance should be part of a carefully
sustained progress rather than a frozen moment.

   All in all, then, the part dominates the whole in *The Saint
and Mary Kate,* and the part that dominates most exquisitely
is character. The strength of this novel is its characters.
Shortly after it appeared O'Connor confessed in a letter to

Nancy, "The older I get the more I love people—all sorts of people, drunk and sober, vicious and virtuous, clever and stupid—particularly the stupid!" He may have hated Cork in general but he loved individual Cork people, particularly the oddities. There is something almost forgivable about Babe McCormick, Mary Kate's overdressed, selfish mother. Her aunt, Dinah Matthews, a charwoman, is the gentle persevering sort of woman O'Connor's mother was, while Mr. Vaughan, Mary Kate's surrogate father, is more than vaguely reminiscent of O'Connor's father—captivating when sober and horrifying when drunk.

However, the two characters, besides the hero and heroine, who are given most memorable life are Dona Nobis and Gregory Mahon, the saintly washer woman and the eccentric carpenter. These two ancients provide the novel with a sort of religious polarity; between her orthodox theological piety and his occult madness. Dona Nobis, Babe's oldest crony, had been affectionately named by her tenement neighbors from a phrase in the hymn she sings continually. Dona Nobis, a pious old maid, knows more about saints and scriptures and less about practicalities and local gossip than anyone else in the tenement. Like the closest friend of O'Connor's mother, Minnie Connolly, her hero is Saint Teresa, from whom, in fact, O'Connor draws this inscription to open the novel:

> Let nothing disturb thee,
> Nothing affright thee,
> Everything passes,
> God is unchanging.
> He who has patience,
> Everything comes to him;
> He who has God,
> He lacks for nothing—
> God, only, suffices.

I suspect that is as close to a religious affirmation as Frank O'Connor ever came, a sort of comic faith in the ability of little people to keep on keeping on in the face of overwhelming adversity. In contrast to Dona Nobis's "library of pious meditations" (87) rest the "mysterious presences" of Gregory Mahon, the old carpenter to whom Phil has apprenticed himself. Saint Joseph had been a carpenter so Phil had to be a carpenter too, and though he eventually masters the mysteries of the trade he can never comprehend the old man's strange belief in three malicious spirits—Felim, Selim, and Thedd. Still, it is Mahon who divines that Phil and Mary Kate have been blown together by the creative force of Thedd: "a white flame of passion must go up from the Marsh, and every sort of amorous allusion was used to incite Phil toward her— without immediate effect" (125). Phil's faith is tested daily by old Mahon, modeled, many Cork people believe, on Daniel Corkery, originally a carpenter by trade. The continual onslaught of Gregory's theology, a combination of rocking– chair philosophy and senile eroticism, creates a religious energy counter to the exaggerated piety of Dona Nobis. The old female saint and the old male romantic mirror the young saintly hero and the young romantic heroine.

Inevitably then, *The Saint and Mary Kate* stands not on its own merit as a novel but on what it reveals about the personal and artistic concerns of Frank O'Connor at the beginning of his career. He was a lyric poet who felt ill at ease behind the mannered mask of verse. He was a storyteller interested more in the flash points of human existence than in the sweeping artifice. And he was a lonely young writer trying to find himself. *The Saint and Mary Kate,* to an even greater extent than his first stories, uncovers the issues, the characters, and the voices that characterize all of his writing: such issues as love, loneliness, and self–delusion; such characters as appear in story after story—little people, innocents, and outcasts, dreamers, eccentrics, and lovers; and the voices of sympathy, of belief, of humor. By the time it appeared in February of 1932, O'Connor confessed to Nancy that his novel had happened to him—"Me as Mary Kate/someone else as the saint."

NOTES

1. See Frank O'Connor, *An Only Child* (London: Macmillan & Co., 1962), chapters 12 and 13, for O'Connor's account of Corkery's influence. "Sion" and "The Peddler" both appeared in 1926 in the short–lived *Irish Tribune*, a Cork weekly which owed a great deal to Corkery and his circle.

2. Isaac Babel, *The Red Cavalry*, trans. Nadia Helstein (London: Alfred A. Knopf, 1929). When Nadia Helstein's translation appeared in 1929, O'Connor ordered it for the Pembroke Library and read the book straightaway, even before processing it for the shelves.

3. Frank O'Connor, *Guests of the Nation* (New York: Macmillan Co., 1931), p. 132. All further references to this work are from this edition and are given parenthetically in the text.

4. Nancy McCarthy was O'Connor's leading lady in the Cork Drama League, and for six years the object of his ardent affections. His letters to her, numbering over one-hundred, are currently in the hands of his widow, Mrs. Harriet Sheehy, who has undertaken the editing of O'Connor's letters.

5. O'Connor's account of his imprisonment forms the final section of *An Only Child*. A more startling and less distilled version, however, appeared nearly thirty years earlier as "A Boy in Prison," in *Life and Letters* (August 1934). Another possible source for "Guests of the Nation," at least in theme, is Thomas Hardy's "The Man I Killed." Hardy, at the time, was O'Connor's favorite poet; he and Yeats often disagreed about the worth of Hardy's poems and his stories.

6. Quoted in *Letters from AE*, ed. Alan Denson (London: Abelard–Schuman, 1961), p. 238, n. 27.

7. Dermot Foley's reminiscences of his friendship with O'Connor appear in "The Young Librarian," *Michael/Frank: Studies on Frank O'Connor*, ed. Maurice Sheehy (New York: Alfred A. Knopf, 1969), pp. 53–63, and in "A Minstrel Boy with a Satchel of Books," *Irish University Review* (Autumn 1974): 204–17.

8. Quoted in *Letters from AE*, p. 238, n. 27.

9. When the Greater Dublin Act of 1931 subsumed such Urban Districts as Pembroke and Rathfarnham in the Dublin Corporation, responsibility for such services as libraries was centralized. Having lost his autonomy, O'Connor gradually lost his enthusiasm; he also lost his assistant, Dermot Foley, a Dubliner who knew all about the bureaucracy of the Dublin Corporation Library Committee.

10. This essay, entitled "Ride to the Abyss," was first sketched out by O'Connor while working on *Dutch Interior* in 1939 and 1940. He later revised it for a Radio Eireann series on Corkery, but decided not to use the material, most of it controversial, in the broadcast. The various versions, in holograph and typescript, remain unpublished and in the possession of Mrs. Sheehy.

11. Frank O'Connor, *The Saint and Mary Kate* (New York: Macmillan Co., 1932), p. 9. All further references to this work are from this edition and are given parenthetically in the text.

Frank O'Connor and The Silence

By Anthony T. McCrann

"You must write poetry as though you were shouting to a man at the other side of the street and were afraid he wouldn't hear you," Yeats once told Frank O'Connor.[1] Sound advice it was and not just as it applied to writing poetry. Silence was repugnant to Frank O'Connor; indeed, he begins *The Lonely Voice,* his study of the short story, by quoting Pascal: "The eternal silence of those infinite spaces terrifies me."[2] In *A Short History of Irish Literature* O'Connor comments on Asenath Nicholson's description of nineteenth-century pre–Famine Ireland in *Ireland's Welcome to the Stranger* (1847): "We realize that debased, hungry and ragged as they were, the Irish were still a race of artists." Whereas Mrs. Nicholson's book "is filled with music and dancing," books describing post-Famine Ireland stress the silencing of the music and dancing which had animated her book; for example, this description by George Petrie of the famine's effects impressed O'Connor deeply:

> "The land of song" was no longer tuneful; or, if a human sound met the traveller's ear, it was only that of the feeble and despairing wail for the dead. This awful, unwonted silence, which, during the famine and subsequent years, almost everywhere prevailed, struck more fearfully upon their imaginations, as many Irish gentlemen informed me, and gave them a deeper feeling of the desolation with which the country had been visited, than any other circumstance which had forced itself upon their attention. [*Short History* 136–37]

113

Seventy some years after the famine we find O'Connor locked up in the Gormanstown prison.[3] He had been imprisoned for his Republican activities during the Civil War and was guarded by other Irishmen—those who had supported the Treaty and the Free State. And what struck O'Connor most deeply during his incarceration?—the silence.

Frank Murphy, another prisoner, had a falling–out with one of the Republican leaders concerning the amount of work he was required to do. Murphy's comrades decided to silence him, to lock him in a hut by himself. Only O'Connor and one other man "talked to him [Murphy] through the bars of his window" (*Only Child* 256). Soon the Republican leadership in the prison convened to discuss more punishment for Murphy. They proposed to boycott him. O'Connor's reaction to this plan to smother Murphy in silence was typical: a vote was taken on the boycott, and when "all those in favour were asked to raise their hands, nine hundred odd hands were raised. When those against were called on, one hand went up, and that was mine. Later in life I realized that it was probably the first time I had ever taken an unpopular stand without allies" (*Only Child* 257).

Later a hunger strike was proposed by the more fanatical prisoners, who urged that none of the prisoners in the country eat until they were released. O'Connor writes: "The idea that thousands of men would keep such a pledge to the point at which mass deaths would threaten the existence of the Free State Government seemed to me absurd" (*Only Child* 265). When O'Connor and a few others resisted, the leadership prevented them from voicing their objections to the majority of the men—"leaving ninety per cent of the prisoners unaware that there were objections to the strike" (*Only Child* 265). O'Connor went to his fellow Cork prisoners to speak against the hunger strike. "I was listened to in silence, and the resolution was passed with only my vote against it" (*Only Child* 266). The strike deadened the prison. It must have been like reliving the Famine:

Most of the hunger–strikers had taken to their beds to keep warm. . . . Partitions and doors had been torn down to keep the stoves going, big cans of water were steaming on the stoves, and the men were lying in or on their beds unshaven, with mugs of hot salt water beside them. . . . But it was the silence that struck me most—all that busy hammering, singing, and chatter ended. [*Only Child* 267–68]

O'Connor himself was silenced, was censored. He was ordered to move into a hut by himself and forbidden to enter anyone else's hut. Finally, some of the men ended the strike; they had been influenced by the silent scolding of the written word: they had read George Russell's "furious" articles in the *Irish Statesman*, in which he had denounced the strike.

O'Connor's life was a long battle against repressive silence, his army drafted from the words which he molded into fiction and hurled thematically at the censors, much as the early *filid* had used their words as weapons against their foes.[4] When he worked for the railway a few years before the Civil War, O'Connor had made a discovery: "All I could believe in was words, and I clung to them frantically" (*Only Child* 170). Later in prison he reflected: "For me, languages had always been a form of magic, like girls, and I would as soon have thought of taking liberties with one as with the other" (*Only Child* 250). Even his political thinking was colored by language, in particular his study of the Irish language: "Whatever the importance of grammar in reading or writing, as an image of human life it seems to me out on its own." He continues:

Maybe it was the grammar that started me off, or maybe the grammar itself was only a symptom of the emergence from a protracted adolescence, but I was beginning to have grave doubts about many of the political ideas I had held as gospel. One was that the Irish Republic founded in 1916 still existed. [*Only Child* 251]

When released from prison, he boarded a train and sat

beside a woman with a baby: "All the way to Dublin J scarcely took my eyes from the baby. . . . All that year I had been missing what Pearse was to remember on the eve of his execution, 'things bright and green, things young and happy' "; and, one adds, things noisy (*Only Child* 274).

The battle between silence and sound, between repression and freedom, had raged long in Ireland and had been renewed in succeeding ages, until, after the Civil War, silence was victorious—in what O'Connor called "a new Establishment of Church and State in which imagination would play no part, and young men and women would emigrate to the ends of the earth, not because the country was poor, but because it was mediocre" (*Only Child* 210).

What was the twentieth–century literary Revival if not an answer to the cultural silence and moribund nationalism? Yeats and his colleagues extolled the peasant, the countryside, the Irish language, and the ancient saga. Born in 1903, O'Connor had grown up alongside the noisy innocence of the Revival. "People took to attending Gaelic League concerts . . . and armed police broke them up. . . . Respectable people . . . [would] walk miles just to attend a concert they were not very interested in. . . . I suspect that in those few years more books were published in Ireland than in any succeeding twenty years (*Only Child* 185–86).

Still, the artists had to struggle for survival even during these fruitful years, from 1900 to 1920. Young Irishmen rioted against Synge's plays. After seeing Synge's *In the Shadow of the Glen* Arthur Griffith exploded: "His play is not a work of genius, Irish or otherwise. It is a foul echo from degenerate Greece" (*Short History* 186). Lady Gregory had declared that the creation of an Irish theater would allow "that freedom to experiment which is not found in theatres of England." About the *Playboy* riots she wrote: "It was a definite fight for freedom from mob censorship." Yet, she and Yeats had been mercurial enough to admonish Synge for writing so much "bad language" in *Playboy*.[5] In spite of these and other conflicts, O'Connor believed the first twenty years of this century to be exhilarating times to live in Ireland.

After the Civil War, however, came a silence which was the result of neither famine nor death. The government–imposed silence of censorship muffled the artists. Brendan Kennelly tells us:

> I think I understood then the sad farce of Irish censorship, the modern middle-class commitment to complacency and swinish apathy, Joyce's nightmare, the ferocious bitterness of many Irish poets and artists I have met, the contemporary fear of the silence of the self.

After hearing O'Connor give a talk on the Famine, Kennelly wrote that he began to understand "the land that rejected its own singers."[6]

Eventually even O'Connor's writing was banned. After the Civil War—the period O'Connor covers in *My Father's Son,* his second autobiographical volume—O'Connor writes that with de Valera's government had come a "new Establishment of priests and politicians."[7] The desire for learning had atrophied. Writing about Osborn Bergin, the great Irish scholar, O'Connor tells us "he was one of the last of a great generation of scholars in a country where scholarship was no longer regarded" (*Father's Son* 109). O'Connor found Irish Studies ignored in Irish universities. When his own work was banned in Ireland, he published in the United States. When his scholarly interests and private life were frustrated in Ireland, he crossed the ocean to teach at American universities. Always the rebel, always loud, O'Connor even rejected the benign coercion of Yeats, his mentor on the Abbey board: "When he [Yeats] began to bully me I always gave him lip, almost on principle" (*Father's Son* 111).

Giving Yeats "lip" was only a continuation of a life–long habit of speaking out. Many critics have noted the "massive contradictions" in Irish writers, and O'Connor is justly cited as a prime example. But there was nothing inconsistent about

his obstreperousness. As a young librarian, he had to fight the
clergy—a clergy whose predecessors had fostered learning:
"Some of the priests would allow no libraries at all" (*Father's
Son* 35). Working as a librarian in Cork, he began a small
dramatic society and found himself and his group attacked for
planning "to produce the filthy work of Sean O'Casey"
(*Father's Son* 60). Years later, when de Valera's government
banned Eric Cross's *The Tailor and Ansty,* O'Connor defended the old couple who had been the book's subject. When
the Tailor and Ansty's story was proscribed as being "in its
general tendency indecent," O'Connor argued against the
ban: "I could say what I liked and did."[8] As one of the board
of directors of the Abbey, O'Connor argued against the plan
of some of the other board members to produce European
classics like *Coriolanus* or *Dr. Faustus,* a policy which would
result in the silencing of Irish talent: "There would be no
opportunity for young serious dramatists. This would mean
the end of the literary movement, for magazine and book
publishers we had none" (*Father's Son* 187).

After Yeats died O'Connor lost hope for the Abbey:
"Mediocrity was in control, and against mediocrity there is
no challenge or appeal" (*Father's Son* 231). O'Connor found
that he must leave the Abbey. He had seen what he felt to be
the silencing of the pantheon of his youth and "was leaving
the theatre of Yeats, and Synge and Lady Gregory, and the
end of their dream of a national theatre that would perpetuate
their work." He could stay no longer where the "terms were
those of the Nationalist–Catholic establishment" (*Father's
Son* 233). To speak out, to challenge the silence, O'Connor
would have to shout, as Yeats had advised. He could no
longer fragment himself by serving on theater boards or other
committees. "At once I resigned from every organization I
belonged to and sat down, at last, to write" (*Father's Son*
235).

Thematically, O'Connor's fiction opposes the many forms
of quietude. One understands that, in a general way, censor-

ship, repression, obsessive sacrifice, martyrdom, death, divisive political factionalism, and even pragmatic reason can be life–denying silences, while spontaneity, creation, imagination, openness, harmony, birth, and children augment sound—at least metaphorically. In particular, O'Connor's fiction celebrates storytelling, dancing, words, language, the ancient oral tradition, and music, all of which rage against the silence.

One of O'Connor's noisiest subjects is the brass band around which the plot of "Orpheus and His Lute" revolves. O'Connor was not unfamiliar with the topic. His father had played a drum in a brass band. "The Cork bands were divided into supporters of William O'Brien and supporters of John Redmond. . . . There were frequent riots, and during election times Father came home with a drumstick up his sleeve." O'Connor's father and most of the other bandsmen had played in the British Army, and "it may have been something of a tragedy to them that when once they returned to Cork, music became less important than the political faction for whom they made it." O'Connor's father was a supporter of O'Brien, but nevertheless spent some years playing for the Redmond band: "It was a superb band, and Father liked music so well that he preferred it to politics." But politics won out—finally he left the Redmond band; "someone in the band must have impugned him by calling him a turncoat" (*Only Child* 6–7).

Even earlier than this, as Malcolm Brown has shown in *The Politics of Irish Literature,* nineteenth–century Irish politics was played to the accompaniment of brass bands. After Daniel O'Connell had caved in to Peel and cancelled the mass meeting which was to be held at Clontarf on October 8, 1843, the Young Irelanders, needing a cornerstone around which they would build Nationalist enthusiasm, teamed up with Father Theobald Mathew, whose solution to Irish drunkenness had been "to organize parish brass bands for teetotalers."[9] At the same time the *Nation* proposed reading rooms, whose focus would be patriotic, "for every parish in the country" (*Politics* 76). When a nationalist insurrection failed in 1848 at Ballingary, Young Ireland was finished. "Bit by bit John O'Connell surrendered the assets of the dead Repeal Association to his creditors: first went the instruments of the brass band, then the library. . . . Once again Ireland found herself at the nadir of the cycle" (*Politics* 114, 116).

The sound from the brass band also symbolized the opposition to nationalism. To counter their fear of Vatican domination in Ireland, "Orangemen came into the streets with their big bass drums." And, on the other hand, George Henry Moore and his group of Irish members of the House of Commons whose goal was to gain Irish demands were christened "The Pope's Brass Band." In 1861 the Fenians organized a mass funeral procession for one of their dead heroes—the march was led, of course, by a brass band. In 1873 an amnesty band which had turned out to help John Martin's election effort in Longford had its instruments seized by young men acting on behalf of the clergy (*Politics* 128, 130, 165, 236). Around the bands, then, swirled Irish factionalism. If there was not lasting harmony, at least there was noisy dissonance, which is better than no sound at all.

O'Connor's "Orpheus and His Lute" is the story of no sound at all. The silencing of the modern artists, the end of the Literary Revival (helped on its way to oblivion by a peculiar new Ascendancy named the Irish Free State), and a new divisive and dominating factionalism (destroying the brief harmonious unity of the 1916 movement), are the foundations upon which O'Connor's story rests.

"Then there was silence," we are told, at the conclusion of "Orpheus and His Lute." The defunct Irishtown Band have peacefully surrendered themselves to prison after playing one more tune—"Auld Lang Syne." "But 'twas funny that they never got the instruments back. They never played again" (*S* 27).[10]

The narrator tells us—and we think of the historical

analogue—that audiences used to support music and cheer for visiting opera companies. "There's no music now like there used to be in the old days. People aren't as keen on it somehow." Fifty years ago, he tells us, there was a kind of harmony: the local band would greet the visiting opera company at the railway station; and even the Church would act in concert with the bands—"Every parish had its band" (*S* 17). But here the narrator is concerned with one particular group of musicians, the Irishtown Brass and Reed Band, and their tale.

The decline of the Irishtown Band is described in language evocative of both the Famine and O'Connor's imprisonment. During practice, the musicians are in great need of drink: "some walking up and down, grinding their teeth, and some lying on the benches, shivering and moaning like men in their last agony" (*S* 19). They send one of their leaders to panhandle for porter at a local pub, and when he returns with an empty jug, the whole band begins to "moan in unison" (*S* 20).

Sowing the seeds of their own downfall, the men decide to load the instruments on a donkey and bring them to old Moon, the Protestant pawnbroker. The winter's night journey to sell out their art is "like a funeral" (*S* 21), like one of those historical marches for the wakes of Irish martyrs, with the musicians serving as keeners. They tell themselves that they will find the money to get their instruments released in time for their Saturday practice. But, as they will later voluntarily enter prison, they now return to their band room and lock themselves in to drink in isolation. By the next night, they have gone through all of the money.

Meanwhile, the other local bands are already practicing for St. Patrick's Day, and the Irishtown's bandmaster, Joe Delury, knows money must be raised to rescue the instruments. But Hegerty, a band member, laments, "I'm afraid our last tune is played." Old supporters offer no help; one, an "old gent who was a great supporter of Parnell," declares: "Ye'll never see a shilling of my money again" (*S* 23). The narrator tells us, "Once people get a notion into their heads that a thing is dead, 'tis damned. Even Father Dennehy, the great priest for the bands, wouldn't give them a hand. He said they were after giving too much scandal." Years later, hearing the silence which had resulted from the turning of the Church and the Nationalists against these imperfect artists, the narrator reflects that if Father Dennehy were still alive, "he might be sorry for giving Irishtown the hard word" (S 24).

By St. Patrick's eve, having only a portion of the needed money, the artists importune Moon to lend them their instruments for a day: " 'You dirty little Protestant scut!' said the bandmaster. 'Hell isn't hot enough for the likes of you' " (S 25). The band's harmonious relationships with nationalists, clergy, and Protestants have been shattered.

Since the Band cannot march, they themselves become silencers. Bitterly jeering at each group of artists, they watch the other bands march. Finally the Irishtown begins a fight with one of its once fraternal, albeit rival groups, the Melancholy Lane Band. They steal the other band's instruments and begin a final march. They confront the civil authority, the police, and are ordered to stop, which they do after playing "Auld Lang Syne." Then there are silence and prison. The police inspector has regretted arresting them: "In my opinion ye're a great band." But that is not enough to save them. They agree to walk to prison peacefully: "We'll finish the way we began, as artists" (S 27).

St. Patrick, the man whose day provides the temporal setting for the demise of the Irishtown Band, was not always an eminence in Ireland. One could say, in fact, that he came to Ireland to silence the indigenous, pagan pantheon; Oisin, for example, is imagined to have survived until the time of Patrick. Away with Niamh in the Land of Youth, Oisin longed to see Finn and his old friends in Ireland. Niamh warned him that "Erin is not now as it was when you left it. The great King Finn and his Fena are all gone. You will find instead of them, a holy father and hosts of priests and saints."[11] When he arrived back in Ireland, he discovered that his old friends were gone, everything had changed, and the country had become the home of little people. The people no longer knew the legends of Finn which the poets had recited. The palace of Oisin's father, Finn, was in ruins and overgrown with grass. Oisin met little men trying to lift a heavy stone, a burden which was too heavy for them, and when he leaned down to help them, his saddle broke, and he fell to the ground, turning into a helpless, feeble, blind old man.

The conflict of artists, pagan traditions, and secularism against Christian religion, then, had simmered for centuries —it was a variation of the battle between sound and silence —but it was not until post-Civil War modern Ireland that, to use O'Connor's phrase, "the Nationalist-Catholic establishment" triumphed (*Father's Son* 233). Sean O'Faolain refers to an early Irish poem, which describes Oisin's reaction upon discovering that Patrick, the new hero, is reigning: "Ah! When Finn and the Fian lived / They loved the mountain better than the monastery."[12] O'Faolain goes on to show that the modern theocracy, with its almost absolute influence over such things as divorce, mixed marriage, birth control, education, and censorship, was a relatively new phenomenon, notwithstanding the fact that Ireland had been a Catholic country for more than a thousand years.

> Although Christianity came to Ireland in the fifth century the Catholic priest, without whom any picture of modern Ireland is unthinkable, does not occupy a central position in that picture until the nineteenth century. The distinction is a political one, for it has to be accepted that what has given the Catholic clergy their social prominence to-day is their political influence, and that without that influence the priest would no more take the centre of the stage in Irish life than does the parson in English life. [*The Irish* 129]

In the nineteenth century, Daniel O'Connell had led the fight for Catholic Emancipation, bringing the priests along with him. By the end of O'Connell's life, the priests were no longer following him; instead, "he found himself being dictated to by the bishops" (*The Irish* 133). The priest was now free and Catholics had the franchise. "This man, who had once been hunted like a wild beast, then barely tolerated, then grudgingly acknowledged as a citizen, was now a power that no local or national politician could ignore" (*The Irish* 134). In the nineteenth century, then, one discovers Cardinal Cullen warning his people on "the subject of literature, a vehicle of sin and infidelity he considered no less dangerous than the mixed colleges." Literature could " 'taint the purity' of believers through the charms of poetic pleasure. The grossest sensualism was abroad, so depraved that it would have corrupted 'even the society of the Pagan world' " (*Politics* 126).

Things were not always thus in Ireland. The eighteenth-century manuscript of "The Romance of Mis and Dubh Ruis," a tale reaching back to early Ireland and describing sexual intercourse as a cure for insanity—intercourse is rather piquantly referred to as "the feat of the wand"—was discovered reposing at, of all places, the Library of St. Patrick's College, Maynooth.[13] In any event, while the Church's power in the secular arena increased dramatically in the nineteenth century, it was not until 1922 that it had instituted itself as the dominant force in modern Ireland. "When a Civil War was raging in Ireland between the 'Republican' forces of Mr. de Valera and the 'National' forces of the Free State Government, the Ordinary of the Diocese of Cork" warned Catholics that shooting Free State soldiers was murder and that priests should refuse the sacraments to disobedient "Republicans" (*The Irish* 139–40). By 1940, O'Connor writes, things had become even worse. "Catastrophe was precipitated by two events that were almost simultaneous—the death of Yeats and the outbreak of the Second World War. Now we had censorship of newspapers as well as censorship of books, and the intellectual darkness of the country was almost palpable" (*Short History* 224).

O'Connor's "Darcy in the Land of Youth" is set in England during the War. The story begins: "One of the few things that Mick Darcy remembered of what the monks in the North Monastery had taught him was the story of Oisin, an old chap who fell in love with a fairy queen called Niamh and went to live with her in the Land of Youth" (*MS* 300). Mick works as a clerk in a war factory in England and is unhappy. Trying to sleep in England is difficult for him: guns and sirens rattle the quiet. And he wonders "what on earth had induced him to leave his little home in Cork, his girl, Ina, and his pal, Chris—his world" (*MS* 301). His silent world.

Liking neither England nor the English, he takes "long, lonesome country walks, but there was no proper country either" (*MS* 301). Then he meets a girl named Janet, who has a "quick-witted laughing air," and who does not "seem to want to convert him to anything, unless it was books, which she seemed to be very well up in" (*MS* 302). Coming home from Janet's flat one evening, he passes some schoolgirls who tease him as they pass: "A bit too broad-minded, thought Mick, coming to himself. Freedom was all very well, but you could easily have too much of that too" (*MS* 303).

Janet soon shocks Mick by telling him that they could be comfortable in her flat if it were not for her roommate, Fanny, and he becomes almost apoplectic when she suggests they spend a weekend together at a country inn. Janet's acceptance of the world "really succeeded in scandalizing him" (*MS* 309). Paralleling Oisin, Mick decides to return to Ireland for his vacation. Although Mick is confused by Janet as Oisin was by Niamh, he knows that she is genuinely devoted to him. But his mind is drawn toward the "nights of tranquil sleep" awaiting him in Cork, beyond "the end of the line" (*MS* 313).

Arriving home, he immediately visits Ina, whom he has been silently betraying. He finds himself changed since leaving Ireland. He shocks Ina's brothers by speaking out, by saying the English probably will not lose the war. He tells his friend Chris, whose conversation extends only to priests and politicians, "You didn't change much anyway." Neighbors stop Mick to ask about "the outside world. Because of the censorship, their ideas were very vague" (*MS* 315). Mick becomes apprehensive—he must either sink into that "tranquil sleep" of Cork or set out again for England. A letter from Janet declares her life is empty without him, but he puts it down without either finishing or answering it. Reflecting on Ireland, he concludes: "People here never talk of anything only religion and politics" (*MS* 316). When Chris counters by saying that at least Mick can sleep here peacefully, Mick shocks him by saying that is only because no woman will ever interrupt his sleep in Ireland.

Mick wants Chris to go to England with him and tells him he has a girl there for him. Abruptly, Mick remembers Janet's unanswered letter and wonders if she meant all that she said. As if waking from a dream like Oisin, Mick realizes that it is Janet who is real. He knows that already he is "thinking in a different language."

> Suddenly he remembered the story of Oisin that the monks had told him, and it began to have meaning for him. He wondered wildly if he would ever get back or if, like Oisin in the story, he would suddenly collapse and spend the rest of his days walking up and down the Western Road with people as old and feeble as himself, and never see Niamh or the Land of Youth.

Finally Darcy breaks the silence. He declares that he has a telephone call to make, and Chris answers, "I suppose you might as well tell her I'm coming too" (*MS* 317).

Returning to England, Darcy had felt "almost as though he were arriving home" (*MS* 318). O'Connor also traveled to England to find a freedom lacking in Ireland, and read aloud his stories on British radio, concentrating on putting the "narrative impulse" back into storytelling. He believed the "written word had robbed the story of its narrative impulse" (*S* vii). But England was not home for O'Connor; Ireland

was, the Ireland of the ninth century and the Ireland of the
Literary Revival. "What I call the period of the Little
Monasteries—the eighth and ninth centuries—is probably the
most delightful in Irish history, at least before the first decade
of the twentieth century" (*Short History* 53). O'Connor's
famous "backward look" was to a far distant past, to an
ancient, vital Ireland of poetry and individuality and imagination and openness. James Matthews writes that O'Connor
found it "significant that whereas Joyce saw in Charles
Stewart Parnell something symbolic of Ireland's search for
itself, Yeats looked instead to Cuchulain."[14] O'Connor believed that his countrymen did not look back far enough—
most focused their visions on the nineteenth century, on
political martyrs and death—while his own imagination
yearned for an ancient, less divisive country; a country which
blended pagan and Christian elements into something all its
own, something very fine.

That Joyce, the *primus inter pares* of great modern writers,
found something symbolic in Parnell is a curious if coincidental coda to the modern malaise, manifested to O'Connor
as silence. Malcolm Brown writes: "Parnell's biographer once
asked Sir Charles Dilke to what he attributed Parnell's success, and Dilke said, 'To his aloofness.' Later he asked a
Fenian, 'What was it about Parnell that struck you most?' He
got the reply: 'His silence. It was extraordinary'." And what
was Parnell's solution for a tenant who was evicted from his
holding and replaced by a new tenant? The interloper must be
left alone and isolated (*Politics* 252, 260). Captain Boycott
learned how potent that solution was when he faced the
"conspiracy of silence."[15]

According to O'Connor, the trouble with Joyce's writing,
and with much of modern fiction for that matter, was its
silence. O'Connor discusses the problem both in *The Lonely
Voice* and in *The Mirror in the Roadway*. In the latter he
writes, "both symbolism and naturalism were a withdrawal
from life."[16] He finds that Joyce's metaphors are concealed.

"This metaphor [in "The Dead"] is unique just because it is hidden. Many nineteenth-century writers, particularly the Americans, used metaphor and allegory, but Joyce's metaphor resembles the dissociated metaphor of dreams, which is intended to baffle and deceive the conscious mind" (*Mirror* 299). Joyce's epiphanies are spiritual manifestations, or quiet nuances. In *The Lonely Voice* O'Connor discusses a popular twentieth-century literary technique which he feels began with Pater and was subsequently adopted by Joyce and Hemingway and their imitators. Their method is one of "simplification and repetition." That is, the same words are repeated over and over again; the writer avoids monotony by employing appropriate forms of the recurrent words to fit changing syntactical slots in his sentences. This repetition, O'Connor writes, "has a hypnotic effect." As the "repetition of key words slows down the conversational movement of the prose," the reader finds himself "falling asleep." Sometimes the effect is not soporific: when Hemingway does not carry the repetition too far, he "rings out loud and clear like music cutting across the silence" (*Lonely Voice* 158–62).

O'Connor's answer is to bring back that loud, human voice to storytelling. Once storytelling had been a public art. Since the modern storyteller "has to speak with a lonely human voice to a private reader," he must bridge the gap between the reader's silent solitude and his own written word" (*Lonely Voice* 13, 107). The short story must again ring "with the tone of a man's voice, speaking" (*S* vii).

Like the tellers of early sagas, O'Connor believed a story is a tale to be told, and it is to be told to an audience. He felt that "Joyce's style is intended to exclude the reader from the action" (*Lonely Voice* 115). As Wayne Booth writes in his discussion of authorial silence in modern fiction, "the author and reader may meet, like Voltaire and God, but they do not speak."[17] If the author and audience do not communicate, obviously the audience is lost, or, as O'Connor puts it, "style ceases to be a relationship between author and reader."

Instead, the author attempts to forge a relationship of a "magical kind" between himself and his creation. Instead of trying to communicate an experience to the reader, the author is interested in "equating the prose with the experience" (*Mirror* 304). One remembers that the dissolution of the Irishtown Band came about simultaneously with that Band's alienating its audience.

"Song Without Words" shows the failure of silent communication; sign-language, a kind of symbolism, is not enough to join Brother Arnold, who "pined for an audience," to Brother Michael (*S* 68). The story is set in a country monastery where the brothers are bound to a vow of silence. Brother Arnold feels the absence of language. Since he has not seen a newspaper in years, he is delighted when Brother Michael lends him some racing papers: "He nearly ate them. Blessed words like fragments of tunes coming to him out of a past life." Even this ersatz literature can stimulate his imagination; remembering a girl he had loved, Arnold forgets her betrayal while recalling "her smile and the tone of her voice" (*S* 69). His memory is flooded by life, music, and sounds. In this silent monastery, however, even the harmless language of the racing papers poses threats. Brother Michael turns his back on Brother Arnold; he leads Arnold to the Prior to confess their guilt. Like the two sides in the Civil War, these brothers are estranged. In suppressing both himself and his friend, Michael has, in effect, imposed censorship on the artist. Arnold had felt the need of an audience. There is none in Ireland.

Whether one reads O'Connor's early or late stories, silence is the villain. Whether one reads stories about children, soldiers, clerics, old people, or adults in provincial middle–class towns, the silence remains the enemy.

O'Connor's "The Idealist" is narrated by a man named Larry, who was once an idealist. As a child he read English school stories from which he extracted a chivalrous code of conduct. The English children in the school stories never lie, whereas Larry's Irish school chums lie continually. Because he often watches British soldiers drilling in the barrack square, he is sometimes late to school. There is only one acceptable excuse for this lateness, a letter from one's mother saying he had been at Mass. The narrator tells us: "The Murderer [the teacher] would never know whether you were or not, and if he did anything to you you could easily get him into trouble with the parish priest" (S 204). Late for school one morning, Larry decides to follow the idealist's code: he decides not to lie. When Murderer Moloney asks why he is late, Larry answers, "I was delayed at the barrack, sir" (S 205). What is worse than the beating administered by the Murderer is his classmates' jeering laughter. Yet, Larry does not flinch. He feels: "If only I could keep my head I should provide a model for the whole class" (S 206).

On the way to school the morning after a subsequent and similar dispute, Larry does not know if he can "face school at all" (S 212). His indecision makes him late, and when Murderer asks him why he is late, he "knew it was no good." "I was at Mass, sir" (S 213). Larry has been silenced, and his attempt at voicing the truth denied.

When O'Connor's characters outgrow boyhood, they often face more sophisticated forms of silence. Mr. Delaney in "The Duke's Children" is an imaginative man, a born storyteller, who turns "every little incident of his day . . . into narrative and drama," but his son Larry is ashamed of his father's storytelling and responds to him with "gloomy silences" (DR 49). Spike Ward, a motor car driver in a small Irish town, is the protagonist of "Don Juan (Retired)" and, like the aforementioned Mr. Delaney, is a vicarious artist and denounced storyteller. Joe French, a local insurance agent, and Jimmy Matthews, the barman at the local pub, find Spike suspect because he has "a good baritone voice which had brought him into contact with undesirables—singers and actors" (MS 113). Spike loves to talk about women, and while the other two men enjoy hearing him, both feel compelled to

attack the storyteller. Time after time Joe and Jimmy fall
under the storyteller's charm and involuntarily function as an
audience. Yet they are also censurious critics, attacking Spike
while titillated by tales that are "in general tendency indecent."

O'Connor does not provide overt portraits of artists' development. Instead, he gives us "laymen" who love sound
and language and narratives. Charlie Ford, the hero of "A
Salesman's Romance," is a "commercial traveller in the
office–equipment business," who by virtue of his imagination
transmutes a typically prosaic occupation, carried on in a
mediocre country, into a work of art. The narrator tells us
that skillful "commercials" are "artists in their own right—
people who make something out of nothing." Charlie's only
flaw, the narrator feels, is that "he could never resist trying to
sell me things, just for practice" (*DR* 186); not just office
equipment, but an idea or even a new self. The pleasure of
creating and then selling his creations, not the money, is what
motivates Charlie.

He is engaged to Celia Halligan, an attractive woman who
has a "cynical but good-humoured contempt for men." Returning one night from a pub in Charlie's car, the couple
crash into the back of a jaunting car which has been travelling
"with no lights on the wrong side of the road" (*DR* 187). The
impact is slight, and the driver—a man named Clarke—is
only thrown forward onto the top of his horse, but he seizes
the opportunity and feigns serious injury. Charlie realizes
that he has "a ripe and subtle intelligence to deal with" (*DR*
188). Clarke, a drunk but creative man in his own way, sues.
And, "as the weeks went by, the jarvey's case grew like a
masterpiece in the mind of a great artist. . . . After months he
was still in bed . . . he got reelings when he rose" (*DR* 189).

As Charlie listens to the subsequent courtroom proceed-
ings, he has a "sudden moment of revelation and joy." He
sees that as audience, the "wretched occupants of the court
were distracted with boredom, and he knew that the only

cure for boredom was to buy something." Charlie decides to sell the spectators something: his own imaginative improvisation (to expropriate the phrase which so often pops up in *An Only Child*). He knows "the whole country was mad with boredom. . . . To express your faith in life it was necessary to buy a stake in the future" (*DR* 193). On the stand, then, Charlie rejects normal courtroom behavior and creates a story no lawyer would buy. As if he were closing a sale, Charlie overcomes Dunn, the lawyer who is questioning him. Charlie creates a drama: he ignores the real questions asked him, and responds instead to questions that have not been asked; he charms the judge; he acts out every little detail of his version of the incident. Like the traditional *seanchai,* smiling and joyful, he turns the entire courtroom into theater and even pleases the crowd by taking swipes at irrelevant subjects such as the "County Council and the condition of the roads" (*DR* 194).

It is, however, one of those fleeting victories of imagination reminiscent of the Republicans' temporary triumph over Britain. It is a meeting of audience and artist and art object. "Charlie, the universal salesman, had sold his story to the jury, and nothing short of an earthquake would break the spell he had woven about them" (*DR* 197). Charlie wins the case but gets little satisfaction from the victory. That night Celia is at a dance with a more kindred spirit, her interrogator, Dunn. And Charlie's victory turns totally to defeat when she returns the engagement ring and says she will marry Dunn. All that Charlie, the artist, has left is the old story: "Out of my great sorrows I made little songs" (*DR* 201).

One could go on and mention any number of stories by O'Connor in which silence, in one way or another, triumphs. In "Uprooted" Ned Keating, a teacher, finds that "the city had failed him" (*S* 75). Tom, his brother, is a priest who feels his life a failure. These exiles undertake a holiday trip to visit their parents' home in the wild countryside. But Ned is no longer at home in his ancestral village, a setting where Irish speakers symbolize ties to the past. He finds himself uncomfortable with his father's songs, spontaneity and openness: "Like a child, the old man loved innocent excitement and revelled in scenes of the wildest passion" (*S* 79). As the sons and their father return from an island where they have spent the day with relatives and friends, the brothers are subdued and silent: "In all the waste of water nothing could be heard but the splash of the boat's sides and their father's voice raised in tipsy song" (*S* 94).

In O'Connor's modern Ireland there is no returning to that sonorous distant past, to the country in which "the Irish were still a race of artists" (*Short History* 136). In "The Long Road to Ummera," an old woman named Abby has to battle her son, Pat, to return to her native village for burial. Like Ireland, Abby is an old woman whose "old heart was failing her." "The rhythm of life had slowed down in her till you could scarcely detect its faint and sluggish beat" (*S* 55). Forty years before, she had travelled the forty miles from the country to the city of Cork with her son. As she waits to die, she talks of "old times in the country and long–dead neighbours, ghosts, fairies, spells, and charms" (*S* 56). Her son, a well-to-do city grocer, hates the "old talk." To Abby, Ummera will be the setting for reunion with her dead husband and friends, but Pat tells her, "That sort of thing is gone out of fashion." To him, Ummera means only "hunger and misery" (*S* 57).

She pleads with him to bury her in Ummera. She reminds him that he had once promised to return her there when the time came. Her son, however, will not help her. She pays Dan Regan, a friend, to drive her to Ummera. Falling ill on the way, she is put into a hospital where an old Irish-speaking priest comforts her. After he promises to have her buried in Ummera, she falls asleep muttering to herself in Irish. Before dying, however, she breaks the silence: "Suddenly Abby's voice rose to a shout and she tried to lift herself on her elbow. . . . 'I'm coming. After all the long years I'm on the road to you at last. . . .' " (*S* 64). She wins; she finally reaches Ummera, but she is, of course, dead.

In modern Ireland there are few Irish speakers with ties to the musical past, either in or out of the clergy. In *A Short History of Irish Literature* O'Connor reminds us that once "Churchmen were treated exactly as though they were poets or druids" (*Short History* 20). He tells us that artists could once rise above political factionalism, reminding us of "the poets' acceptance of the Norman invaders and their readiness to write poetry for them exactly like the poetry they wrote for native chiefs" (*Short History* 90). About the more recent past, Vivian Mercier writes, "An audience consisting mainly of older people would gather in some hospitable house around a turf fire to listen until bedtime to one or more storytellers" (*Great Stories* 10). Mercier also comments on O'Connor's insistence that "the written word had robbed the story of its narrative impulse." What O'Connor meant, Mercier feels, is "that the short story had lost its dramatic quality, its spontaneity, the sense of a man telling a story to other men. It must be remembered that the traditional storyteller was allowed some scope for spontaneity and individuality" (*Great Stories* 14–15).

Concomitant with the Gaelic language revival was Yeats's ascension to primacy among Irish writers. O'Connor believed one of the keys to Yeats's success had been his talent for "placing the dull word, the commonplace phrase to restore the tone of the human voice speaking" (*Short History* 178). O'Connor had a powerful voice and tried to capture both the spontaneity of earlier storytellers and the natural human voice he had found in Yeats when, after Yeats's death, he read his own stories on British radio.

He did not read them on Irish radio. He was censored in his own country. In 1909 Shaw had given Lady Gregory *The Shewing up of Blanco Posnet,* his play which the British censor had rejected. Lady Gregory writes: "Mr. Shaw offered us the play for the Abbey, for the Censor has no jurisdiction in Ireland—an accidental freedom" (*Theater* 140). When the British authorities in Ireland tried to halt the play's production anyway, Lady Gregory said: "We did not give in one quarter of an inch to Nationalist Ireland at *The Playboy* time, and we certainly cannot give in one quarter of an inch to the Castle." She went on, reminding the Castle officials, that neither did she "give in to the Church when Cardinal Logue denounced the *Countess Cathleen*" (*Theater* 155). Irish writers had stood up to the Nationalists, the Church, and even the British, once. What a sad irony, then, that by the early 1940s Irishmen, not the English, were muffling O'Connor. He had, of course, escaped to England. Maybe Mick Darcy was right when, ruminating in "Darcy in the Land of Youth," he concluded, "Happiness, that was the secret the English had and the Irish lacked" (*MS* 321–22).

The silence remained O'Connor's lifelong adversary: historically, artistically, and personally. The modern Irish proclivity for discussion of religion and politics resulted only in discordant noise. Irish passion had been deadened. O'Connor returned regularly to Ireland from abroad. Like Father Devine in "The Shepherds," he was coming back to the "prison-house of his youth" (*MS* 257). And, like Oisin, he saw little men carrying a great burden: men who would not attend the burial of Douglas Hyde, the President of Ireland and founder of the Gaelic League, because Hyde was a Protestant and Catholics were no longer allowed to attend Protestant funerals (*Short History* 228). O'Connor believed himself one of the "strayed revelers of the Irish literary revival, and by the early 1940s this was all over and done with" (*Short History* 229). In his "Light Dying: In Memoriam Frank O'Connor (Michael O'Donovan),"[18] Brendan Kennelly writes:

> I hear you now, your rich voice deep and kind,
> Rescuing a poem from time, bringing to mind
> Lost centuries with a summoning word,

....

Or else you cried in rage against the force
That would reduce to barren silence all
Who would articulate dark Ireland's soul.

NOTES

1. Frank O'Connor, *A Short History of Irish Literature: A Backward Look* (New York: Capricorn Books, 1968), p. 178. Hereafter cited parenthetically in the text as *Short History*.

2. Frank O'Connor, *The Lonely Voice: A Study of the Short Story* (New York: Bantam, 1968), p. 9. Hereafter cited parenthetically in the text as *Lonely Voice*.

3. Frank O'Connor, *An Only Child* (New York: Alfred A. Knopf, 1961), pp. 256–68. O'Connor's perceptions of the attitudes of the prison camp described in subsequent paragraphs are drawn from this passage. The volume is hereafter cited parenthetically in the text as *Only Child*.

4. Vivian Mercier, *The Irish Comic Tradition* (New York: Oxford University Press, 1969), p. 107.

5. Lady Gregory, *Our Irish Theater* (New York: Capricorn Books, 1965), pp. 9, 115, 133. Hereafter cited parenthetically in the text as *Theater*.

6. Brendan Kennelly, *Selected Poems* (New York: E. P. Dutton, 1972), p. xi.

7. Frank O'Connor, *My Father's Son* (New York: Alfred A. Knopf, 1969), p. 129. Hereafter cited parenthetically in the text as *Father's Son*.

8. Eric Cross, *The Tailor and Ansty* (Cork: Mercier Press, 1972), p. 7.

9. Malcolm Brown, *The Politics of Irish Literature: From Thomas Davis to W. B. Yeats* (Seattle, Wash.: University of Washington Press, 1972), pp. 74–75. Hereafter cited parenthetically in the text as *Politics*.

10. O'Connor's short stories will be cited parenthetically in the text by an abbreviation and page number(s) which refer to one of these editions:

  S   *Stories by Frank O'Connor* (New York: Vintage, 1956).

  MS   *More Stories by Frank O'Connor* (New York: Alfred A. Knopf, 1954).

  DR   *Domestic Relations* (New York: Alfred A. Knopf, 1957).

11. Mary McGarry, *Great Folk Tales of Old Ireland* (New York: Bell Publishing Company, 1972), p. 93.

12. Sean O'Faolain, *The Irish: A Character Study* (New York: The Devin-Adair Company, 1949), p. 21. Hereafter cited parenthetically in the text as *The Irish*.

13. Vivian Mercier, ed., *Great Irish Short Stories* (New York: Dell Publishing Company, 1964), p. 32. Hereafter cited parenthetically in the text as *Great Stories*.

14. James H. Matthews, *Frank O'Connor* (Lewisburg, Pa.: Bucknell University Press, 1976), p. 28.

15. Joyce Marlow, *Captain Boycott and The Irish* (New York: Saturday Review Press, 1973), p. 149.

16. Frank O'Connor, *The Mirror in the Roadway* (New York: Alfred A. Knopf, 1964), p. 189. Hereafter cited parenthetically in the text as *Mirror*.

17. Wayne C. Booth, *The Rhetoric of Fiction* (Chicago: The University of Chicago Press, 1961), p. 272.

18. Kennelly, *Selected Poems*, pp. 24–25.

Esther Waters: An Irish Story
By Wayne Hall

In May 1899 the co-directors of the Irish Literary Theatre,
W. B. Yeats, Edward Martyn, and George Moore, officially
launched their organization with performances of Yeats's *The
Countess Cathleen* and Martyn's *The Heather Field*. Although the event signaled the start of a brilliant period in Irish
drama, it seemed at the time more noteworthy for the various
quarrels within the literary movement that began boiling over
into public controversy. Yeats's play had come under attack
as heresy and an outrage against Catholicism; Martyn, himself a strong Catholic, then considered withdrawing, not only
his own work, but also his financial backing so badly needed
by the enterprise. In the end, Martyn's religious qualms could
be mollified, and attempts to disrupt the performance of *The
Countess Cathleen* remained small and manageable. The only
major participant somewhat disappointed by this restoration
of harmony was George Moore—Martyn's cooperation had
deprived him of the occasion for a revealing essay on Martyn
and his "Soul." Further occasions for skirmishes with friends
soon followed, however, as when Martyn huffishly refused to
accept Moore's revisions of his play *The Tale of a Town;* or
when Yeats, against Moore's threats of a legal injunction,
appropriated one of their joint plots for the play *Where There
Is Nothing;* or when, in 1902, the Irish Literary Theatre itself
broke up, with Moore feeling himself excluded from its
successor, the Irish National Dramatic Company. A few

years later the first rumors started to circulate nervously through Dublin that Moore was gathering material for a satiric, probably even slanderous, chronicle of the Irish Renaissance. By the time the first volume of this work appeared in 1911, Moore had prudently departed for London, his original vision of becoming Ireland's cultural messiah transformed into his epic masterpiece of mock-heroic irony and gossip, *"Hail and Farewell!"*

For all its brilliant criticism of the movement to which Moore himself belonged, *"Hail and Farewell!"* added but one more side to the whole range of complicated ambivalence in his long relationship with Ireland. Outraged by the Republican forces who in 1923 burned Moore Hall, his family's manor house in County Mayo, he would later write, "No country is so foreign to me as Ireland. . . ."[1] A similarly clean separation of sensibilities from his country of origin had earlier allowed him to claim *Esther Waters* (1894) as an "English" novel. Yet the same affection for Moore Hall that turned to bitter grief at its destruction also binds *Esther Waters* to his family estate. Although set in England and concerned with the life of an English servant woman, the work takes its most powerful substance from experience that is uniquely Irish. It not only dramatizes, several years before Moore heard of such a thing as a national theatre, the state of mind that eventually drew him back to Ireland and its blossoming literary movement; the novel also helps to identify some of the main feelings underlying that artistic renaissance and to locate those feelings within particular transformations of the Irish political, economic, and social structures.

Esther Waters describes what happens to a person who attempts to succeed, in the way that would make her happiest, within a society that precludes success and streaks of luck. Not visibly in a state of decline itself, the society of the novel nevertheless inexorably forces each of its characters into failure and hardship. They have no way of reversing their fates and can at best only recognize the futility and irrelevance of action in the face of such complex and powerful environmental forces. Those desires for happiness that depend on outside means inevitably end in ruins. People find contentment, Moore suggests, not by seeking external success, but by turning inwards, beyond the range of action. As she comes to rely less and less on a society that takes more than it gives, Esther finally rests upon the simple and life-sustaining core of her personality, one too solid for the world to break. Yet even when defined on her own terms, her character emerges primarily from the experiences of deprivation, calamity, and loss. The answers she gains for herself demand a withdrawal from and rejection of the world in which she has found little more than suffering.

In exploring the theme of defeat in the world of action and society, Moore took up problems that grew out of his own roles as both a novelist of insecure financial and aesthetic means and the landlord of a large estate in late nineteenth-century Ireland. The novel's depictions of the emotions and consequences of failure draw much of their immediacy of feeling from his anxieties about his status within the circles of artistic talent and landed power. Moore Hall faced the same economic pressures threatening thousands of large Irish estates at that time: how to control its own fortunes during the major social transition that was increasingly eroding the wealth, power, and privileges of the landed gentry in Ireland. Although he never approached Esther Waters's extreme poverty, Moore well understood the fear of one day ending up with nothing and the desperate hope of somehow breaking into the streak of fortune that would reverse the decline.

Badly shaken by the sudden news of Moore Hall's possible financial collapse, he returned to Ireland from Paris in 1880, more conscious than ever of the dilemma confronting his landed class. In *"Hail and Farewell!"* a mysterious "voice" called him home from London in 1901, not to a failing manor house this time, but to a cultural revival that was in part a response by the artists to the perceived decline of their society. *Esther Waters* comes directly between these events. In its concern with the theme of failure, the novel points towards both the plight of the Big House and the lost cause mystique cultivated by the Renaissance writers. The sort of ambivalence that marked Moore's attitude towards the artistic movement, as in his disappointment over Martyn's cooperation with the Literary Theatre, appeared similarly in his view of his own class in his alternate repudiation of and then identification with the gentry. In the fictional world of *Esther Waters*, which emerges as a further attempt to answer his own personal Irish question, Moore sought to resolve the uneasy union of decadent aesthete and cautious, sensible landlord, to balance his desire to escape from his point of origin against his need to return to it.

He left Ireland in 1873, as soon as his twenty-first birthday gave him the option of life in a country less hostile to art. His father, George Henry Moore, parliamentarian, landowner, and racehorse enthusiast, had died three years earlier, ostensibly of a stroke; but he had been seeking to break a threatened rent boycott in the final days of his life, and his son George felt quite sure who bore responsibility for the family's loss: "He died killed by his tenants, that is certain; he died of a broken heart."[2] In 1880, widespread agrarian unrest fostered by the Land War again raised the spectre of ruin for Moore Hall; his land agent's letter to Paris warned of an imminent crash and crystallized all of Moore's worst fears about the downfall of everything he valued.[3] He saw himself thrown back upon an as yet untried and not very lucrative talent, condemned to pander to the philistines for his very survival. Throughout the 1880s and early 1890s, his art gained for him no financial security, no tangible proof of his worth as a writer, no comforting release from anxieties about a surly tenantry and a weak and ineffectual landlord class. Moore Hall did continue to produce a modest income, but Moore frequently worried that the tenants might at any time capriciously refuse to pay and so plunge him into debt.

Seeing his own class as a debased, weakened, and paralyzed remnant of its former nobility, Moore portrayed many of his fictional characters during these years as likewise debilitated by some defeat. If the position of the landed gentry in Ireland was indeed hopeless, if decisive action and committed heroism could make no difference, then the man of sensibility had best learn to face the collapse of his world. Such feelings of determinism would eventually lead Moore away from the earlier characterizations and towards his creation of Esther Waters, whose nature allowed him both to depict accurately the hopelessness of her position and still to keep her immune from the horror of failure or mediocrity. Within the universal spiral of decline, the individual could find personal salvation only by renouncing the need for success and by turning inwards upon a life-sustaining simplicity. For Esther, defeat on the world's material terms would not mean failure but rather a return to more enduring spiritual values.

Esther Waters is Moore's best-conceived treatment of the experience and emotions of failure, and one of the best novels by an Irish writer. In this work, action becomes irrelevant, success only a transitory illusion, society an unbeatable opponent in a series of wagers that are destined to come up empty. Unlike the other characters in the novel, however, Esther manages to free herself from a reliance on external supports and from the irrational and desperate hopes for a reversal of fate. Finally outside of the constricting pressures that Moore felt surrounding him, she gains an enviable position through her return to and complete acceptance of simple and fundamental beginnings. And insofar as Esther represents Moore's concept of an idealized self, the novel offers one more form of the autobiography that continually occupied him during his career.

Moore first touched on the subject matter for a novel like *Esther Waters* when he commented on a charwoman in the *Confessions of a Young Man* (1888): "And I used to ask you all sorts of cruel questions, I was curious to know the depth of animalism you had sunk to. . . . I merely recognise you as one of the facts of civilisation."[4] By 1889, the idea of the servant woman had assumed more artistic and economic relevance; he wrote of a forthcoming shift in the tone of his fiction, with which he hoped to achieve greater success: "My next novel . . . will be more human. I shall bathe myself in the simplest and most naive emotions, the daily bread of humanity."[5] His attitude of condescending superiority and emotional distance could only sustain itself as long as the novel remained an abstract calculation, and by the time he came to write the final pages, Esther's story had aroused feelings in him far deeper than those aimed solely at the marketplace: "For the first time in my life I cried over my work."[6] In Ginger's hasty and grudging visit to his mother at Woodview in the final chapter, especially when contrasted with Esther's loyalty and devotion to her place of origin, Moore must have recognized his own errant nature.

In drawing on specific features of his Irish experience for *Esther Waters*, Moore had several character models at hand, as well as the details from his father's stable-yard. Mrs. Barfield, the mistress of Woodview, has the same simple morality, piety, and patient kindness that Moore's mother showed. Both women remained on their respective estates, even after their husbands had died, their sons had moved away, and their manor houses had decayed into shadows of an earlier splendor. Woodview itself resembles in its externals a Sussex home where Moore occasionally visited during his first ten years in London. The interior of the estate, however, closely copies Moore Hall, especially the stable area. And as he noted in *"Hail and Farewell!"*: "At Moore Hall there was no life except the life of the stable-yard, and to it I went with the same appetite as I went to the life of the studio after-wards. . . ."[7] Much of the stable-yard excitement of his youth revolved around the butler, Joseph Appley, and his small, cluttered, but sacrosanct office, or "press." Like his novelistic counterpart John Randal, also called Mr. Leopold,

Appley cultivated an aura suggesting encyclopedic knowledge and secret systems, all guaranteed to identify prospective
race winners. Moore later reminisced about "that wonderful
press in which all things could be found. It was out of that
press that *Esther Waters* came, out of the stable-yard and out
of my own heart."[8] Appley aroused considerable admiration
in the young George Moore; but what he represented, the
horse-racing and the betting, elicited only hostility and re-
sentment from the women of the manor.

Although *Esther Waters* describes the life of the large city
as well as that of the country house, Janet Dunleavy points
out that the details of Esther's experiences in London are not
as accurate as the accounts of the racing stables and the
Woodview estate. Esther's journey on foot to get a letter
recommending her for admission to a lying-in hospital, for
instance, would hardly have been possible in the time Moore
gives her.[9] He directs his richest and most vivid attention, and
most of the informed and realistic description, towards the
world of the stables and the races. What he did not personally
observe in his first twenty years he could absorb from the
involved reports of the servants. Just as Esther missed "Silver
Braid's" race, the nine-year-old Moore did not see the victory
of his father's horse "Croaghpatrick." But the family and
servants could talk of nothing else for weeks, especially as the
huge winning purse of £20,000 had signaled an ascent in
Moore Hall's previously unsteady fortunes.

Woodview estate likewise undergoes periodic shifts in its
economic status. The Barfield family three generations before
had worked as livery-stable keepers. Under the previous
squire, they finally rose to the level of a "county family" and
still keep that title, despite the socially questionable marriage
of the present Mr. Barfield to the daughter of one of his
tenant farmers. The string of racing victories temporarily
silences the local gossips and, in fact, raises the wealth and
esteem of the manor to its greatest height. Yet the personal
history of the Barfield's cook, Mrs. Latch, suggests the

inevitable reversal of those fortunes dependent on the luck of the races. Her husband, better off than the Barfields at one time, lost heavily through betting; now, Mrs. Latch's son William represents the family's hope for a restoration of the old fortune. Within the treacherously shifting cycle of family destinies, however, by the time William can build up a prosperous business, the Barfields have suffered heavy betting losses, and Mr. Barfield has died of a "broken heart."

Esther comes from a much simpler family background. She belongs to the Plymouth Brethren, an ascetically puritan, fundamentalist Christian sect that allows no pictures, ornamentation, or even prayer books into their worship. She and her mother share the same pious religious beliefs within their "narrow, peaceful family life."[10] Required to stay at home and help her overburdened mother, Esther never learned to read, although she still carries her mother's few books with her throughout the novel. In her first days at Woodview, she is awed by the romantic world that emerges from a trivial magazine story read by a fellow servant. Print for her appears mysterious and fascinating, but also threatening; her religious instincts win out, and she denounces the story as sinful and corrupting.

In her dealings with the rest of the world, Esther maintains the perpetual stance of the adversary, and "it was only when she laughed that her face lost its habitual expression, which was somewhat sullen . . ." (p. 1). She must constantly fight to control her quick temper and her open suspicion of other people, seeing anger as not only a personal weakness, but also a threat to her survival. Throughout the novel Esther feels the need to restrain herself, to shape her nature and her desires through an act of will into those habits she instinctively believes they must take. Only when her desires correspond to the simplicity of her instincts can she feel completely happy.

The novel repeatedly contrasts desire with instinct. Desires are capricious and transitory, directed towards external objects or goals, provoked by society, and consequently subject to social disappointment and frustration. Instinct, on the other hand, remains fixed and unchanged, the essential core of a person's nature within the erratic flux of his desires. Much like conscience, instinct grows out of ingrained habits of thought that one can trust much more than illusory, worldly desires. Connected to nature, it need not depend for its fulfillment on social gratification or success. Moore believed that "in Esther Waters I represented a woman living in the deepest human instincts."[11] In the *Confessions* he related the concept of instinct to the semi-mystical echo-auguries that periodically led him to further stages of his artistic development: "brain instincts have always been, and still are, the initial and the determining powers of my being."[12] If a person could maintain his awareness of those instinctive powers, Moore suggests, he could more easily recognize what in his life would bring him a measure of happiness and contentment. By giving way to whims and desires, by acting against conscience and instinct, a person separates himself from his internal being and leaves himself at the mercy of external rewards. Implicit and consistent faith in one's instinct offers a much more reliable guide to conduct.

Moore structures the entire novel around such a dichotomy—the opposition of desire and instinct, the external world and the internal self, sense and spirit, complexity and simplicity. One way, the way of desiring the attractions of the world, raises people's hopes and lures them into an active involvement with life. The other, instinctive and religious, seeks through a withdrawal from the world to find contentment in an inner-directed state of mind and a simpler range of human needs. In the course of Moore's novel, Esther alternates between these two poles and finally reconciles them into a stable synthesis. With action leading to nothing but failure and defeat, and outward success offering only fleeting satisfactions, she can find happiness only through a retreat inwards, away from the world and towards her natural instincts. Within the overwhelmingly complex and deterministic social forces outside her, desires turn to frustrating illusions. By at last coming to rely on her inner nature, by wanting only a simple existence and no more, she brings desire and instinct into balance. There, Moore would have it, does she win her salvation.

Mrs. Barfield experiences the same feeling of opposition between desire and instinct that Esther does. Also a member of the Plymouth Brethren, she becomes Esther's friend and confidante and tries, with meager results, to teach Esther to read; with similar patience and results, she also seeks to win her husband away from the influence of his butler and the world of betting and racehorses. The lure of a bet infects almost everyone in the novel. It reassuringly promises an end to insecurity and fear of deprivation, a beginning of pleasure in a life that otherwise seems like a deadening cycle. One great stroke of luck could transform a life, or so a person irrationally hopes. But insofar as the hope depends on external success, it has no chance of effecting any significant change or of bringing any substantial happiness.

As an analogue to Moore's own experience, betting on horses resembled a gamble on the literary market. His economic dependency on his early writing forced him to try for potential winners by predicting the response of critics and the reading public. At the same time, however, he could paradoxically only regard such a gamble as doomed to failure. If an artist reduced his work to such a calculating and mechanistic level, Moore believed, he would produce inferior art; if he ignored the taste of the marketplace, he would not sell. The dilemma was compounded even further by Moore's own partial success and by his awareness of the economic straits of the landed gentry in Ireland. If decisive action had no influence on such external circumstances, whether as a bet on a horse, or a wager on the literary field, or a responsible attempt to restore the family estate, then Moore could explain to himself his own choice of art, a profession that offered no support to the decaying fortunes of Moore Hall.

For Esther, betting represents only the most obvious side of a whole range of experience she speaks of as the "world." And the world extracts one concession after another from her as she feels alternately attracted to, and then threatened by, contact with the life around her. Since life, in Esther's view, harbors mostly immoral temptations and false rewards, her instincts eventually force her to suspect anything nonspiritual that she finds enjoyable, such as the richness and novelty of her experiences at Woodview. Her seduction by William Latch and resulting pregnancy only confirm to Esther the original premises of her religious outlook. Released from Woodview with very little money and no prospects for further employment during her pregnancy, she believes she can only thank God she has not suffered still more for her sin. The pattern repeats itself over and over for Esther: she accepts from the world, then her instincts reassert themselves, and so she rejects what she has desired and taken, sees it as one more temptation leading to moral depravity.

After nine years of desperate poverty and isolation, with only her child for comfort, Esther eventually meets William again, and this time he wants to marry her. She still finds him intensely attractive, partly because he belongs to the Woodview experience, which "had become the most precise and distinct vision she had gathered from life" (p. 205). She spends several prosperous and happy years with William, and together they build up a thriving business from his tavern and an illegal betting operation. Despite the good fortune of this period of her life, however, Moore depicts almost nothing of these years except for a panoramic recreation of a great Derby. For him, Esther's character can best emerge from her times of hardship and ruin; the material comfort and success seem irrelevant. He thus passes over the good years with more tragic accounts of minor characters, especially of Sarah, whose life closely resembles Esther's at many points. The striking parallels between their respective fates suggest that Esther's happiness rests on very fragile ground.

The disasters begin to pile up. William contracts tuber-culosis, which reduces his gambling to its most elemental level; his life literally rides on each succeeding bet as he desperately tries to raise the money needed to take him to a warmer climate. As he has done throughout his life, he struggles against fate, attempts to control it himself. But the futile hopes for a winner get played out for the last time in the novel, and William's death leaves Esther at much the same level of poverty as before her marriage: "Horses had won and horses had lost—a great deal of trouble and fuss and nothing to show for it" (p. 330). Esther married William partly out of economic motives, and after his death some of her thoughts about him resemble regret over a bad investment. From the beginning she has unfailingly kept her son Jackie as her first love, despite her attraction to William, and in her son she now takes her comfort.

More than anything else outside her, Jackie determines Esther's character in the novel. Even when William lies dying, she realizes that "her boy was what was most real to her in life" (p. 337). She builds her strength on that belief, and on her determination to smooth out Jackie's future as much as possible and shield him from anything unpleasant. Her heroism is defined in large part by her blinding concern for her child, and her characteristic gesture remains one of stoical and withdrawn silence; she withholds from Jackie even the news of his father's impending death.

From the moment she first knew of her pregnancy, most of Esther's life has centered around her son. Neither William, nor Fred (a deeply religious Plymouth Brethren member who wishes to marry her), not even her own religion, ever absorbs as much of her emotions and conscious thoughts as Jackie does. When she decides on various courses of action, she does so with an eye to what will benefit him most. Moore reserves his most sentimental passages to describe their relationship, but despite the Pre-Raphaelite silliness that occasionally cloys his point, he gives Esther's character the necessary depth through her sacrifices for Jackie. In the realistic context of her hardship and suffering, she does take on the status Moore accords her: "Hers is an heroic adventure if one considers it: a mother's fight for the life of her child against all the forces that civilisation arrays against the lowly and the illegitimate" (p. 163). The claims for universality, romantically overblown in this statement, take on genuinely far-reaching implications in the whole of the novel. There, all human endeavors face the same one-sided struggle, regardless of the limitations of poverty or birth.

Because Jackie exists, Esther must commit herself to action. He, more than anyone or anything else, prevents her from retreating from the external world back into her private, inner nature and self-sufficient isolation. From the time of his birth he gives her something outside herself to relate to: "Her personal self seemed entirely withdrawn; she existed like an atmosphere about the babe, an impersonal emanation of love . . . unconscious of herself. . . ." (p. 118). As Jackie draws her out into the world, he helps make possible all the other compromises Esther must reach with the instincts that would lead her back to shelter. Through Esther, therefore, Jackie provokes the novel's ultimate test of the worth of human endeavor. If action is indeed useless, even at its most elemental level, then human life is useless, and birth does little but add to the world's wretchedness. Moore rejects such nihilism throughout the novel as well as in the closing pages. But he cannot entirely control the uncertainties of feeling in the final chapters, the difficulty of withdrawing from a world that remains vital and attractive despite its universal chronicle of failure.

When Esther finally returns to Woodview, she feels sensible of nothing but the comfort of a total retreat from the world. While Woodview has changed drastically since she left, she concentrates almost entirely on those things that have remained unchanged, even obliterating from her consciousness the events of the intervening eighteen years. All that time seems "now a sort of blur in her mind—a dream, the connecting links of which were gone. . . ." (p. 365). Mrs. Barfield has stayed on alone at Woodview, just barely able to maintain the estate, but still willing to offer Esther the shelter both women accept as the final stage in their lives. In her return to her beginning, Esther retreats into the comforting reassurance of words she heard from Mrs. Barfield in her first years at Woodview: "time has passed like a little dream; life is nothing. We must think of what comes after" (p. 318). In the experience of the novel, however, Esther only superficially turns to the redemptive possibilities of a Christian heaven. Moore's own skepticism about religious beliefs kept him from attempting to depict complete faith in an afterlife and led him instead to seek a resolution in the context of this world. Esther's thoughts thus remain primarily with life, though one that has now become internalized and spiritual, insulating her against the external world. She finds contentment by rejecting the complexity and materialism of the world outside Woodview, the world that so often seems to her like a dream, and by reducing her human needs to a minimum.

When Esther had to decide whether to marry William or Fred, she had a dream in which the two men merged into one ideal personality. Woodview for her closely approximates such a combination of their best qualities. She can enjoy the peace and spiritual confidence of her religious faith without Fred's aggressive dogmatism. And she has the minimal material pleasures and security that William offered her without having to wrench her moral instincts into an acceptance of the tavern and the betting. She also has William's son, who becomes an important concern for Mrs. Barfield now as well. The older woman too had to tolerate her husband's betting habits, and with Esther, she now seems happiest with life at Woodview without the interference of husbands. The simpler and more pure relationship of mother and child resolves the difficult complications of marriage.

In *Parnell and his Island* (1887), Moore described two Irish manor houses, both falling into neglect and decay, shabby cast-offs from an earlier brilliance. One of them, Moore Hall itself, was still inhabited by George Moore's mother. In many of the details and in the atmosphere of melancholy ruin, Woodview closely resembles these estates. Moore also uses recurring notes within the novel itself to add to the dream-like mistiness of the final pages. In relating Esther's return, he repeats almost word for word several sentences that opened the novel with her first arrival at the train station.[13] The cyclic pattern emphasizes what has endured at Woodview, not what has gone, as if to say that the intervening years and changes did not really matter.

Mrs. Barfield's son Ginger makes one of his rare visits to Woodview soon after Esther's return. A gentleman jockey with a small training stable in the north of England, he shuns his home estate while still demanding that it maintain the proper shabby-genteel decorum. He thus becomes enraged on learning that his mother conducts prayer meetings there with people he considers a bunch of petty "shopkeepers." Mrs. Barfield responds, not with argument or protest, but with a patient and simple explanation of her faith: "An expression of great beauty came upon her face, that unconscious resignation which, like the twilight, hallows and transforms. In such moments the humblest hearts are at one with nature, and speak out of the eternal wisdom of things" (p. 369). Shamed by his unfaithful criticism, Ginger leaves the women to their own affairs. In comparison to his mother's transcendent and visionary happiness, his own life suddenly appears to him shallow and crudely business-like. It does not occur to him to measure his own loyalties against Esther's; yet by resurrecting such a relatively minor character at this crucial final stage in the novel, Moore implicitly compares the two, and in the process, seeks to resolve some of his own guilt. Much like Ginger in the avoidance of his home, Moore partially absolves himself of disloyalty by creating an idealized child like Esther, one who returns to her beginnings, who stays on and responsibly cares for the family, who may even miraculously save the estate from sinking further into the general cycle of decline and ruin that depletes the fortunes of the gentry.

As with Ginger's sudden doubts about the worth of his life, the uneasiness Moore felt for having abandoned Ireland and the family estate were complicated by uncertainty about his own artistic talent. Despite fears of personal poverty and scorn for a peasantry he considered hardly better than savages, he appreciated the privileges offered by the immense distance between landlord and tenant. If he would not rightfully earn those privileges by staying in Ireland and managing his family's estate, then the burden fell on him of creating great art, of contributing to the spiritual growth of society as the peasants contributed to the material. Trapped within the ambivalence of his position, Moore could only go on collecting rents from afar and hoping for some satisfactory resolution through his art. And all the while, his recognition of the repressive injustice of the whole landlord-tenant system kept adding to his anxieties about artistic failure. Dependent upon the tangible financial success of his work, Moore could constantly see before him in these early years the economic connection between his function as unproductive landlord and as the artist who had yet to prove he could produce. The threats of a land-hungry peasantry were not too far removed from those of an unresponsive reading public.

Esther's son Jack also returns to Woodview at the close of the novel, with more self-assurance than Ginger can muster, but his visit presents Moore with other artistic problems. Seeing her son in his handsome soldier's uniform, Esther feels only pride and affection and quite naturally does not imagine the battlefield dangers he might have to face or remember the hardships he caused her as a child. Given the bleak novelistic universe Moore has created, we as readers, like Esther, have no logical reasons for supposing that Jack's fortunes will turn out any better than those of the other characters. Each of them, in his or her ambitions and conduct, ended with little but failure and the knowledge that such ambitions and conduct prove ultimately futile. Yet we do not think Esther blindly optimistic or foolish in her hopes for her son's success in the world. Like a great horse race, the world that Jack has grown into remains an attractive and tempting possibility; even if the bet is irrelevant and hopeless in fact, it does not always seem that way in fancy. The vitality and fascination of the world beyond Woodview continue to raise Esther's hopes for her son. But Moore instead puts more artistic commitment into the only other alternative the novel holds out against despair: the kind of retreat Esther chooses for herself.

The final stage in Esther's life does not carry enough conviction, does not ring true enough with what has come before, to carry the universality with which Moore would burden it. Insofar as Esther's solution negates experience, it becomes unacceptable outside her own life, even in a world that irresistibly contaminates action and turns it to failure and ruin. Her happiness on returning to Woodview is too much a negative happiness, the relief one feels when the pain and suffering finally stop. Moore claims much more for it than that in attempting to create a positive ideal. He would have Esther discover a transcendent state of mind in which wisdom and contentment, instinct and desire, merge into one complete whole. And he would locate this discovery in the process of withdrawal, as thorough as possible, from the external world. The final sentence of the novel retreats even further towards an inner quietness and self-sufficiency, beyond the demands of time and space: "And in silence they walked toward the house" (p. 377). The simple conjunction "and," with its feeling of seamless narrative and continuous gesture, adds the final shadow to the twilight veil of timeless and unchanging beauty. Esther pulls back into her characteristic silence, needing only the presence of the two people she loves in the house of her origins.

It all looks too much like death and a denial of the earlier experience. In the vital realism of the stables and the races, Moore created a life that here resists such annihilation. He wishes to refine Esther into an ideal, one who, because of the external limitations of her unique social status, can look at the world out of a deep, elemental simplicity and thus attain a vision of basic and eternal wisdom. She is a person who has "accomplished her woman's work" (p. 377) and a servant who still retains the customary social distinctions with her mistress long after these courtesies have lost their social meaning. She comes from the lower classes and ends in more acute poverty than when she began. And perhaps most important as a recurring motif, she cannot read. Malcolm Brown believes that "Esther's illiteracy seems to have symbolized for Moore a sort of primordial, almost protoplasmic, strength which would survive all persecutions and outlive her persecutors. . . ."[14] Esther has kept her mother's books throughout her life away from home, but shortly before she returns to Woodview even those are stolen from her. Print becomes unnecessary and would, in fact, corrupt her through information, through its exposure of the complex and fatally alluring outside world. But we do not think of Esther as fundamentally different because of her illiteracy, her sex, or her social status. All of Moore's characters share in the common experience of failure and defeat. Esther's particular response to her disasters may not be as uniquely ideal as Moore claims. Her retreat into peace, silence, and simplicity may rather be very human weakness, an understandable exhaustion with the world, an acceptable desire just to withdraw from it all.

If we as readers cannot take Esther's final stage as a response to emulate, Moore himself had even greater difficulties. Esther is about thirty-eight when her story closes. At that age, Moore was beginning to turn over in his mind the ideas for the novel *Esther Waters,* a book that would bring a solid measure of success to a career that would last four more decades. His next major heroine, Evelyn Innes, would retire from the world because of too much commercial and artistic success, not because of too little. With his mother's death in 1895, Moore could more easily accept his decision to leave Moore Hall behind him. While she kept the estate alive, however, and while he still feared he might fail utterly as an artist, Esther Waters, the ideal child, could resolve some of the guilt and insecurity of George Moore, the ungrateful son. Loyal to her beginnings, beyond the need for good fortune, she seemed to Moore truly to have found happiness. She represented a return to the simplicity of an earlier age, a time before the politicians, the demands for land reform, the agrarian agitation, and the weak and compromising landlords had begun to shift the balances in Ireland. The undeniable loss of that age contributed to Moore's depiction of Esther within a general environment of defeat and ruin. Yet he also hoped to find that a spiritual return to simple beginnings need not end in a void, that individual human character might still succeed where history had gone frighteningly wrong. Moore may have wished to become such a person as Esther himself, but it was not even remotely possible.

NOTES

1. Joseph Hone, *The Life of George Moore* (New York: Macmillan Co., 1936), p. 383. This is the standard biography of Moore to date, although a new biography has been undertaken by Hilary Laurie. Hone's *The Moores of Moore Hall* (London: Cape, 1939), provides additional historical information on the estate and on Moore's family.

2. Maurice Moore, *An Irish Gentleman, George Henry Moore* (London: T. Werner Laurie, 1913), p. xx.

3. Malcolm Brown, *George Moore: A Reconsideration* (Seattle, Wash.: University of Washington Press, 1955), p. 15, says of the letter from Joe Blake, the land agent: "The traumatic shock of Blake's letter was the most memorable experience of Moore's life."

4. George Moore, *Confessions of a Young Man* (London: Sonnenschein, 1888), p. 213.

5. Moore to Clara Lanza, in Hone, *Life*, p. 161.

6. Moore to Lena Milman, November 1893, in Helmut E. Gerber, ed. *George*

Moore in Transition: Letters to T. Fisher Unwin and Lena Milman (Detroit, Mich.. Wayne State University Press, 1968), p. 80.

7. George Moore, *Vale*, vol. 3 of *"Hail and Farewell!"* (London: Heinemann, 1914), p. 25. The first two volumes from this trilogy, all first published by Heinemann, are *Ave* (1911) and *Salve* (1912).

8. Moore, *Vale*, p. 25.

9. Janet Dunleavy, *George Moore: The Artist's Vision, the Storyteller's Art* (Lewisburg, Pa: Bucknell University Press, 1973), p. 109. Dunleavy provides one of the rare views of *Esther Waters* as an "Irish" novel. Brian Nicholas, in "The Case of *Esther Waters*," in *The Man of Wax: Critical Essays on George Moore*, ed. Douglas A. Hughes (New York: New York University Press, 1971), p. 178, expresses the more common view when he writes that "the melodramatic conception of virtue . . . has involved Moore in a full-scale portrait of a woman with whose ideals he has nothing in common, who is to him essentially indifferent."

10. George Moore, *Esther Waters* (London: Walter Scott, 1894), p. 21. All further references to this work are from this edition and are given parenthetically in the text. Moore issued revised editions in 1899 and 1920 and a uniform edition in 1932. His dramatization of a portion of the novel appeared as *Esther Waters* in 1913. Royal A. Gettmann, in "George Moore's Revisions of *The Lake, The Wild Goose*, and *Esther Waters*," *PMLA* 59 (June 1944): 540–55, discusses the revisions of the novel. In summary, Gettmann finds that scarcely twenty pages remain unaltered, yet "in narrative method, theme, and purpose the novel remains unchanged . . . the work of a competent craftsman patching surface details" (p. 555). He claims the style becomes smoother and more colloquial and that the novel is presented more from Esther's point of view. Many of the stilted or redundant or simply pompous passages have been removed; some exposition is recast into dialogue; and many of the short, choppy sentences are combined into longer ones.

11. Moore to Lena Milman, Summer 1895, in Gerber, ed., *George Moore in Transition*, p. 110.

12. Moore, *Confessions*, p. 38. Moore borrowed the phrase and the idea of "echo-augury" from Thomas De Quincey.

13. In later editions, Moore omitted the second group of sentences as perhaps too mechanical a literary device.

14. Brown, *George Moore*, p. 133.

The Good Shepherd and the Anti-Christ in Synge's *The Shadow of the Glen*

By Thomas J. Morrissey

During the half hour or so that it takes to perform *The Shadow of the Glen,* the audience is likely to laugh at the foolish antics of Dan Burke and his protege Michael Dara, sympathize with Nora Burke, Dan's lonely and unappreciated wife, and wonder at the Tramp's verbal dexterity. The comedy is readily discernible: no one can miss the humor in Dan's pretended death or in Michael's groveling before the suddenly risen dead man whose wife he has been wooing. Although the pathos of Nora's situation is also apparent as a result of her poignant speeches, the play's deepest moral and philosophical implications are imbedded in a rich matrix of what Nicholas Grene calls the "complex and subtle patterns" that audiences are apt to overlook the first time around.[1]

One serious and subtle pattern that complements even the most farcical elements of the plot arises from Synge's persistent and often ironic use of Biblical symbolism, a tactic which he employs later in *The Playboy of the Western World.* His use of the New Testament in *The Playboy* is the subject of several commentaries, most notably Stanley Sultan's "The Gospel According to Synge,"[2] but the role of the Bible in *The Shadow* has not been explored. Raised in a strict Protestant home, Synge was intimately familiar with scripture, more so than most members of his Catholic audiences. Consequently, despite the fact that biblical allusion is a major vehicle in the play for the playwright's heretical ideas on religion and politics, it was Nora's possible adultery, not Synge's blasphemy, that angered Nationalist critics when the play was first performed in 1903.[3]

Synge uses the Bible to give mock mythic significance to the comic action of *The Shadow of the Glen*. He creates his own version of the primal Christian myth—the death and resurrection of Christ—in which the nominal Christians, Dan and Michael, become purveyors of spiritual death, while the antiestablishment figures, Patch Darcy and the Tramp, become prophets of a creed that preaches a life–oriented gospel of spiritual and material liberation. In the context of this myth, Nora's choice is clear: she can opt for stagnation or freedom. At the same time, the irony is heightened by the fact that although Synge clearly identifies Darcy and the Tramp with Jesus and the Apostles, he does not allow his vagabond evangelists, however Christian they may be in spirit, to preach a doctrine of life after death; thus Synge leaves in doubt the precise nature of Nora's salvation.

Synge's use of the Bible highlights the differences between two pivotal characters, Dan Burke and Patch Darcy. In the mythic scenario, Dan is a comical but potentially vicious anti-Christ who exemplifies the concept of death-in-life. Doubtless a professed Christian, Dan adheres to a selfish and highly judgmental value system. Patch Darcy, the well-meaning half-mad shepherd, embodies the concept of life-in-death. His ethical trademarks are generosity and self-sacrifice.

The most obvious irony surrounding Dan's feigned death is that Nora can find little difference between him dead or alive. Emotionally and sexually, he was always moribund, as she say while "looking uneasily" at his body: "Maybe cold would be no sign of death with the like of him, for he was always cold, every day since I knew him—and every night. . . ."[4] As

Nora comes to realize, life with Dan is the equivalent of psychological death.

The surface humor is enriched by Synge's depiction of Dan as a distorted type of Christ. Dan's pretended death and resurrection constitute a parody of Christ's passion and rising, a parody which is the basis of the comic debasement of Christianity as practiced in Wicklow. Like Jesus, Dan suffers, though in a far less dignified manner, and, when his passion leads to death, the earth becomes dark. Nora says,

> Then he went into his bed and he was saying it was destroyed he was, the time the shadow was going up through the glen, and when the sun set on the bog beyond he made a great lep, and let a great cry out of him, and stiffened himself out the like of a dead sheep. [35]

In Dan's case, death is contingent on the darkness, rather than the other way around. His last cry is as unintelligible as Jesus's last cries are meaningful (Luke 23:34, 43, 46). Jesus dies only once, but Dan is temporarily revived by the desire for whiskey (43). When he does momentarily arise, he tells the Tramp, "Let you wait now a short while, and it's a great sight you'll see in this room in two hours or three" (43). This statement echoes Jesus's words to the disciples, "A little while, and ye shall not see me; and again, a little while, and ye shall see me, because I go to the Father" (John 16:16). Dan has no intention of going to the Father; the great sight he envisions is more reminiscent of the Christ "who shall judge the quick and the dead at his appearing and his kingdom" (2 Tim. 4:1). When the mock savior finally arises, Michael Dara crosses himself uttering the ejaculation, "Son of God deliver us"; however, since Michael is primarily concerned with allaying Dan's wrath, his prayer is addressed to the pseudo-Son rather than to the real one. Finally fulfilling his role as celestial judge, Dan condemns Nora for her sins.

Dan's ploy is not depicted in religious terms solely for comic effect. The farcical similarity between his acts and those

of Jesus is an ironic commentary on the hypocritical self-
righteousness of the religion which permits his actions.
Though Jesus is supposed to have died to redeem sinners,
Dan dies to punish them, specifically his wife. Neither Dan
nor the audience knows for certain whether Nora has been
unfaithful to her husband, but Dan would punish her for
having even a Platonic male friend. Like the wrathful God of
judgment, he commends Nora and Patch Darcy to the devil
(43), but since he cannot wait for either God or Satan to inflict
punishment, he throws Nora out of the house, knowing that
the fear of religious and, ultimately, economic sanctions will
prevent Michael Dara or anyone else from helping her.
Synge's ironic use of religious symbolism suggests that by
passing judgment Dan is usurping a divine function. The fact
that Michael is not compassionate enough to save the woman
reveals that society as a whole shares Dan's ethical outlook
and therefore condones the persecution in life of those alleged
sinners who might perhaps be more justly rewarded in the
hereafter. Thus, the spiritually moribund Dan Burke is only
as dead as the religious milieu in which he lives, a fact which
places Irish Christianity in direct opposition to the more
tolerant creed of Dan's spiritual counterpart Patch Darcy.

In contrast to Dan the anti-Christ, the late Patch Darcy
exemplifies life-in-death. While living he was active and vital,
and would "run from this to the city of Dublin and never
catch for his breath" (47). Sedentary Dan Burke spends his
life "thinking thoughts in the dark mist" (35). Patch offered
Nora a welcome respite from boredom, which is why she
says, "it's very lonesome I was after him a long while" (39).
Unlike Dan, whom Nora and Michael Dara forget immediately, Patch lives on in the hearts of those who loved
him. According to his friend Michael, Dan's greatest gifts to
mankind are a sock full of money and a timely passing (51). In
contrast, Patch's legacy is his memory, in supreme tribute to
which Nora says, "he was a great man surely, stranger, and
isn't it a grand thing when you hear a living man saying a

good word of a dead man, and he mad dying?" (47) Thus, while Dan pretends to be dead though alive, there is a sense in which Patch can be said to be living though dead.

Synge gives religious significance to Darcy's life-in-death status through the use of biblically inspired sheep and shepherd symbolism. This motif identifies Patch with Jesus the Good Shepherd. Pat Barnett demonstrates how the sheep symbolism reveals the characters' relative closeness to nature and how it shows that "Darcy is directly opposed to Michael."[5] In fact, the sheep motif reveals that Patch is philosophically opposed to both Dan and Michael. The sacrifices Darcy makes for his sheep are much like those made by the biblical Good Shepherd. Nora says that he "would walk through five hundred sheep and miss one of them, and he not reckoning them at all" (47). The Tramp amplifies the image when he says that "there was never a lamb from his own ewes he wouldn't know before it was marked, and he'ld run from this to the city of Dublin and never catch for his breath" (47). Indeed, Darcy dies in the rain with his sheep while each of them coughs and chokes "like an old man" (39) as if in sympathy. These passages clearly identify him with Jesus, who says of himself:

> I am the good shepherd; the good shepherd giveth his life for his sheep./ . . . I am the good shepherd, and know my sheep, and am known of mine./ . . . My sheep hear my voice, and I know them, and they follow me./ And I give them eternal life. . . . [John 10:11, 14, 27–28]

Nora and the Tramp love Patch Darcy for his vitality and devotion to his flock; these are the very qualities that Jesus attributes to the only kind of shepherd worth following. Both Darcy and Jesus know their sheep and would spare no effort to save them, including death. Darcy is Christ-like in his spontaneous outpouring of love and as such is the polar opposite of Dan Burke, the anti-Christ. Patch Darcy's madness is no impediment to his deification, for, like Jesus, he

espouses beliefs that run contrary to those of people who
might be described as eminently sane and practical.

Thus Synge uses sheep symbolism to contrast the self-
sacrificing shepherd with the self-interested Michael Dara.
The Tramp's description of Michael as a "poor herd" causes
the young man to admit his failings in a way which defines his
alienation from nature and the Good Shepherd archetype:

> It's no lie he's telling, I was destroyed surely. They were that
> wilful they were running off into one man's bit of oats, and
> another man's bit of hay, and tumbling into the red bogs till it's
> more like a pack of old goats than sheep they were. Mountain
> ewes is a queer breed, Nora Burke, and I'm not used to them at
> all. [47]

Michael cannot control his sheep because they do not recognize his authority nor does he know anything about their
behavior. Thus the mutual knowledge which characterizes the
relationship of Patch and Jesus to their sheep is totally absent
in the case of the bad shepherd. Furthermore, Dara is not only
unwilling or unable to sacrifice for his sheep, but he also
expects them to sacrifice themselves for him. He tells Nora,
"I'm no fool now at making a bargain when my lambs are
good" (51). His interest in his sheep is purely mercantile.
Darcy undoubtedly sold his sheep for slaughter too, but his
interest in them was not strictly pecuniary. Dara, therefore,
views nature as a thing to be passionlessly exploited, which is
symptomatic of the kind of man who would marry a widow
for her money and then reject her for fear of social ostracism.
His rapacious capitalism and blind adherence to the religious
status quo are implicitly condemned by Synge's use of sheep
symbolism.

The title of the play echoes the "shadow of death" of Psalm
23 of the King James version. Although Dan's feigned death
is the focal point of the comedy, real death, as symbolized by
the shadow of the glen, is what Donna Gerstenberger calls the
"ultimate defeat" that nature inflicts upon man.[6] Each of the

contrasting Christ figures offers a way of dealing with the lethal umbra, and it is between these ways that Nora must choose. Dan's and Michael's absorption with material wealth cannot satisfy Nora, for she has been exposed to the rod and staff of Patch Darcy. Her spiritual rejection of her husband occurs when she first befriends Darcy and takes solace from his company. So antithetical are the opposing philosophies of life that Dan must disown Nora without being sure that she has been unfaithful sexually.

The Gospel of Patch Darcy according to the Tramp contains the only hope of escape from psychological death, but it offers no relief from physical death. The major difference between his example and the teachings of Jesus is that Patch Darcy does not promise eternal life. He can protect his sheep only as long as he is alive. The significance of this is that Nora and the Tramp are inspired by the memory of Darcy's devotion, not by hope of reward. While Darcy cannot give immortality, his memory celebrates the principle of loving sacrifice, thus giving his human followers the strength they need to face the shadow of death in a more positive manner.

Darcy's leading spokesman is the Tramp, whom Synge characterizes by means of both the Biblical sheep symbolism and a complementary motif, that of the "good tailor." These motifs underscore the compatibility of the Tramp's every action and speech with Darcy's philosophy, but they do so in a gentle and often humorous way. The good tailor mends his coat while dispensing wisdom, occasionally in the form of sarcasm and wit. When Michael calls him a "poor tailor," he responds as befits a follower of the Good Shepherd, saying, "If it's a poor tailor I am, I'm thinking it's a poor herd does be running back and forward after a little handful of ewes" (47). This is a meaningful retort given the importance of competent shepherding in the play. Elsewhere, in a moment of good humor, the Tramp makes light of having to sit alone with Dan's body: "I'd be putting a little stitch here and there in my old coat, the time I'll be praying for his soul, and it going up naked to the saints of God" (41). The Tramp's whimsical comment demonstrates his balanced approach to life. Unlike Michael, who is totally devoted to the here and now, he tends to his basic physical needs while offering a token prayer for Dan's immortal soul. He can afford to be humorous because he has already learned enough about Dan to suspect that perhaps his soul is beyond mortal help.

The Tramp's sewing is the primary background activity during his initial conversations with Dan and Michael. In contrast, much of the subsequent action, including Nora's memorable speeches on the horrors of old age and death, is punctuated by Michael Dara's covetous counting of Dan's money. These parallel background activities accentuate the philosophical differences between the creeds of Darcy and Burke. Like Darcy, the Tramp performs necessary labors without complaint; like Dan Burke, Michael rejects all emotion and sentiment in favor of exploitation and acquisition.

Within the context of Synge's reconstructed Christian myth, the Tramp offers Nora a chance to experience what is worthwhile in the world, at least as long as she is able to do so. The famous speech in which he promises that she will hear "the herons crying out over the black lakes" (56) is an invitation to explore nature in his company and with the guidance of God, or at least some kind of metaphorical natural spirit. The nature imagery of his last speeches is as vivid as that of Psalm 23. The follower of Darcy, the Good Shepherd, bids Nora to follow him into Darcy's natural world. The fact that his leader died in madness is not important to him because the quality of Darcy's life while sane is the only viable alternative to psychological death. If one cannot ultimately escape the shadow of death, one can avoid entering it prematurely by leading a life of hope and vitality.

Synge's Biblical symbolism is doubly ironic. First, it affords him one more device through which to discredit Irish religion and politics. As Robin Skelton observes, "Synge's detestation of modern capitalist society was as strong as his distrust of religious dogma"[7]; hence, it is only fitting that as spokesmen for a heartless bourgeois Christianity Dan and Michael are laughable failures. The Biblical motifs, with their profound philosophical implications, give additional moral force to Synge's partiality to Darcy's ethical system. A professed socialist,[8] whose admiration for Wicklow's vagrants is well known, Synge writes to Molly Allgood (Maire O'Neill):

> I dont fit well in to that family party somehow, they are rich and I am poor, and they are religious and I'm as you know, and so on with everything. . . . Success in life is what they aim for, and they understand no success that does not bring a nice house, and servants, and good dinners.[9]

At the same time, however, Synge's deification of Patch Darcy is tongue-in-cheek. If Christ, the judge, can drink whiskey and shake a big stick, the Good Shepherd can die mad in a ditch. Synge's aversion to Christianity is strong enough that he does not choose to make Darcy a completely serious Christ figure. Also, his idealization of the Tramp, which Harold Orel points out is not especially realistic,[10] is not to be taken as absolute truth within the context of the play. Synge avoids being too specific concerning what gifts the Tramp offers Nora. As Jean Alexander asserts, Nora joins the Tramp "in full knowledge, without illusion."[11] Gérard Leblanc makes a perceptive point when he writes in his article on Synge's ironic reversals: "Nora is not taken in by the Tramp's lyricism but she will take the risk in order to escape a life where material security and moral conformity have been substituted for imagination and emotional fulfillment."[12] The Tramp is a congenial and gifted conversationalist, not a wild-eyed prophet. His rescue of Nora is as playful and fanciful as Synge's use of the Bible. If, as Donna Gerstenberger[13] and others have claimed, Nora's leaving with the Tramp is less than believable given the realities of peasant life in rural Ireland, then perhaps the use of the Bible to depict Dan as an unendurable spiritual pervert is designed to give

Nora sufficient justification. Still, the spectre of toothless Peggy Cavanaugh haunts Nora as she takes to the roads, and it may be said with some justice that the play's tonal ambiguity is never fully resolved. It is equally possible that what appears to be ambiguity is really ambivalence on Synge's part. His own view of the world is close enough to that of Patch Darcy to make him highly sympathetic to the exiting vagabonds; however, like Nora, he questions the Tramp's undiluted optimism. The sight of Dan and Michael—the play's spiritual bankrupts—drinking whiskey together as the curtain falls should be enough to cause an audience to join Synge in hoping that there is, after all, something substantial in the Tramp's symbolic evangelism. By pitting a humorous type of Christ against a farcical anti-Christ, Synge strikes at the heart of bourgeois Christianity in Ireland. He is, as Seán McMahon puts it, "a siren voice of freedom"[14] calling out against the dominance of the church and the economic system. At the same time, however, the heroes of *The Shadow of the Glen* are gentle parodies of Christ and his followers, so that in the play and, very likely, in the mind of the playwright, Christlike values, rather than Christian dogma, remain intact.

NOTES

1. Nicholas Grene, *Synge: A Critical Study of the Plays* (Totowa, N.J.: Rowman and Littlefield, 1975), p. 97.

2. Stanley Sultan, "The Gospel According to Synge," *Papers on Language and Literature* 4, no. 4 (1968): 428–41.

3. For Nationalist reactions to the initial performances see Lennox Robinson, *Ireland's Abbey Theatre: A History, 1899–1951* (London: Sidgwick and Jackson, 1951), p. 36.

4. J. M. Synge, *The Shadow of the Glen*, in *J. M. Synge: Collected Works*, ed. Robin Skelton (London: Oxford University Press, 1962–1968), vol. 3, *Plays*, ed. Ann Saddlemyer (1968), p. 35. Page numbers are hereafter cited parenthetically in the text.

5. Pat Barnett, "The Nature of Synge's Dialogue," *English Literature in Transition* 10, no. 3 (1967): 120.

6. Donna Gerstenberger, *John Millington Synge* (New York: Twayne Publishers, 1964), p. 43.

7. Robin Skelton, "The Politics of J. M. Synge," *Massachusetts Review* 18, no. 1 (1977): 18.

8. Ibid., p. 11.

9. J. M. Synge, *Letters to Molly: John Millington Synge to Maire O'Neill,* ed. Ann Saddlemyer (Cambridge, Mass.: Harvard University Press, Belknap Press, 1971), p. 13.

10. Harold Orel, "Synge's Concept of the Tramp," *Éire-Ireland* 7, no. 2 (1972): 55–61.

11. Jean Alexander, "Synge's Play of Choice: *The Shadow of the Glen,*" in *A Centenary Tribute to John Millington Synge, 1871–1909: Sunshine and the Moon's Delight,* ed. S. B. Bushrui (New York: Barnes & Noble, 1972), p. 30.

12. Gérard Leblanc, "Ironic Reversal in Theme and Technique in Synge's Shorter Comedies," in *Aspects of the Irish Theatre,* ed. Rafroidi, Popot, and Parker (Paris: l'Université de Lille III, 1972), p. 55.

13. Gerstenberger, *John Millington Synge,* p. 40.

14. Seán McMahon, " 'Leave Troubling the Lord God': A Note on Synge and Religion," *Éire-Ireland* 11, no. 1 (1976): 140.

Bloom Among the Orators: The Why and the Wherefore and All the Codology

By Fritz Senn

Most of us take delight in the well-turned phrase. Eloquence is a virtue in many cultures, like the two that interest us here, the world of the Homeric epics and of Joyce's (but not only Joyce's) Dublin. *Ulysses,* in one of its many ways, brings the two together; the novel seems to assemble a more than average proportion of gifted speakers into its relatively narrow confines. These speakers find various pretexts to pass the time of day and night in loquacious company, and Joyce helps them in aligning a series of scenes in public houses or in pub-like constellations—a newspaper office, a library, a maternity hospital room or a cabman's shelter, all of which can turn into the setting for a contest in verbal skills. *Ulysses* is full of talk and much of it may sound like talk for talk's sake. Don't let us forget that the one conspicuous narrative deviation on the first page of the novel, that metathetical word and name "Chrysostomos," re-Hellenizes "golden mouth" as a traditional figure of speech for men who had a way with words.

No one is safe from the lure of the spoken word. Even as aloof a person as Stephen Dedalus is "wooed by grace of language" (140[1]). Nor is he immune to the even greater temptation—in the library episode—to display his own superior mastery of words and Shakespearean diction. Dubliners excel in talk and enjoy it; they are moreover competent judges of each other's performances. *Ulysses* contains many comments on the language of its protagonists. Even Molly Bloom, not Dublin's foremost intellectual, has been endowed with a shrewd sense for the wrong or pretentious note.

Skillful speakers, like tenors, are admired and successful. The performance itself can be more important than any information conveyed or idea presented. The glib talker, whatever his level, can usually make it through the day and at least get his drinks provided for. Lenehan is a case in point: "his adroitness and eloquence had always prevented his friends from forming any general policy against him," we learn in *Dubliners* (*D* 50) and find this comment confirmed in *Ulysses*, where he is still able to market a limited stock of witticisms, no matter how much the worse for wear, to his own best advantage. The stories in *Dubliners* highlight types who know how to turn a phrase and get on in the world, such as Gallaher in "A Little Cloud," with "his fearless accent" (*D* 70) and his memorable "sayings" (*D* 73). By 1904 he is still held out as a model for, of course, journalism. From all we know of Corley in "Two Gallants," he may not have much to say, but apparently he can say it with aplomb and it works well enough. Mrs. Mooney, of "The Boarding House," is full of confidence; she has social opinion on her side and the right arguments, but also, we can assume, she will know how to reexpress them properly. Other characters remain tongue-tied and self-conscious. Thomas Malone Chandler only wishes "he could give expression to" his emotions (*D* 73), but clearly will never think up Byronic cadences; and no matter how he tries on rare occasions, he will never sound like a man of the world in a public bar. A man like Farrington in "Counterparts" is miscast in a job which depends on copying words and sentences, and in a crisis he lacks the wit to cope with it verbally. When his tongue finds what he takes to be "a felicitous moment" (*D* 91)—and it looks like a fairly unique event—the words chosen actually precipitate his downfall and their first result is "an abject apology"; that is, the instant annulment of those words. Gabriel Conroy's superiority in "The Dead," such as it is, is also due to his command of words that suit the occasion. He can confect a speech, with allusions and quotations, and the speech is adequate (most likely he will be asked to speak again next year); his reputation is confirmed. Conversely, when he fails with words (as he thinks), he is disconcerted, afraid he may have "taken up the wrong tone." His accomplishment may be reinterpreted as "orating to vulgarians" (*D* 220), but, for all practical and public purposes, the power of words *is* an asset.

Among the hierarchies within *Dubliners* there is one that is rhetorical. This is seen best in the oratorical rivalry among the visitors of Mr. Kernan, in "Grace," with the lower ranks vainly striving for attention and acknowledgment. The story appropriately begins with a defective tongue and culminates in the glib speech of a professional preacher with "resonant assurance."

Lily, the caretaker's daughter, is right: "The men that is now is only all palaver" (*D* 178). And it is largely palaver that men are judged by.

The tale of the *Odyssey* can be interrupted in praise of the man who has a way with words, and this is often its hero. The preeminence of Odysseus in verbal as well as practical resourcefulness has led one classical critic—the only one to be mentioned in *Ulysses,* and that in the chapter which deals with rhetorics—to claim that the initial epithet, *polytropos* (*Od.* 1. 1), suggested the hero's ability to utilize "many tropes," that is the whole arsenal of rhetorical tricks.[2]

This semantic twist is doubtful enough, but the linguistic cunning of Odysseus needs little demonstration. It is established in his first speech, a sceptical reply to the nymph Calypso. The reply is introduced by the common formula "*epea pteroenta*," to alert the listener to the "winged words" which will follow. After them the nymph at once comments upon what he has said and how he has said it. "Thou that hast conceived and spoken such a word" is the stilted version of Butcher and Lang for the original

hoion de ton mython epephrasthes aqoreusai [*Od.* 5. 183]

which is, literally, something like: "Such a *mythos* (= word, saying, tale, fable) have you thought up to say aloud (publicly)." The point is that before the painful moment of parting, the goddess takes time out to remark upon the quality of the speech and to review it as a significantly clever example. We notice, by the way, that Dubliners too have a penchant for judging words and speeches.

The first spoken words of Odysseus are sandwiched between *"epea pteroenta"* and *"hoion mython,"* and even if Joyce never looked at the original, it is interesting that *epos* and *mythos,* both terms that primarily referred to the act of speaking, have come to stand for important concepts, important for Homer's art and for Western culture. Joyce's *Ulysses* has helped to redefine their meaning.

Naturally the novel plaits a tag like *"epea pteroenta"* into its texture: "the winged speech of the seadivided Gael" (324). This phrase has become proverbial (Homer uses it more than a hundred times), almost the prototypical cliché, the kind of thing that Joyce tends to assimilate into his work both as one of the many literary comedowns, the timeworn and overused set pieces that have become unfit for any other than parodistic use, *and* in its (once) metaphorical aptness and precision. For "winged" sets words off from the more pedestrian duties that they normally perform. It signals occasions for them to soar above quotidian banalities.

As it happens, "winged" (or *pteroenta,* from *pteron,* feather) suggests that to parts of language can be attached what Joyce's first acknowledged patron saint in an emergency fixed onto himself. This is a procedure which, as we know, calls upon some ingenuity and has its inherent risks. The Daedalus myth, as built into *A Portrait* (where the image of a "winged form," *P* 169, is stimulated inter alia by the contemplation of the poise, balance, and rhythmic rise and fall of words, *P* 166–69, and where language itself, in accordance with myth-inspired ecstasy, begins to take off from the ground) and into *Ulysses,* implies both the success and the Icarian variant of failure. The hazardous plight of words engaged in ecstatic flight contributes much to the Joycean comedy of incongruities. There can be a rhetorical *hubris* too, an attempt by language to overreach, aim too high. For example, the speech by Dan Dawson, as reported in "Aeolus," accumulates altitudes like *"serried mountain peaks"* and is in itself *"towering high on high"* (125), but there is one short step from *"overarching"* to *"overarsing"* (123).

Ulysses begins on a raised platform, with a sustained showpiece and recital by the most accomplished orator and impersonator of them all, Buck Mulligan of the golden mouth and the inexhaustible (though perhaps, in the long run, slightly repetitious) repertoire. Never at a loss for the right word, he usurps many of Stephen's roles of priest and bard and also, at one turn, provides himself with wings. With "his hands at his sides like fins or wings . . . fluttering his winglike hands" (19), he proclaims his ascension in a Daedalus-cum-Christ routine while doing an Icarian caper down towards the sea. From the start he links up with the classical tradition, uses familiar Homeric tags and invents Homeric types of epithets. He generally finds a trope for every ploy. With his rapid changes of voice and act he is indeed, as a later parody has it, "mirth-provoking," and causes "considerable amusement" (307). One would naturally invite him to one's party, as George Moore does later in the day (and the exclusion of Stephen Dedalus, with his cryptic utterances and sullen asides, is understandable too). Mulligan is a worthy successor of Mahaffy and Oscar Wilde, a voluble quoter and himself eminently quotable. There is hardly a reader who would not remember the Buck's first words, spoken aloud, and ceremoniously. At least we remember that the Latin of the Mass is mockingly misappropriated.

The extroversatile Buck heralds Ulyssean techniques and a Homeric role which is to be played in a more modest key, and much more fumblingly, by Leopold Bloom, who has inherited some of the scepticism, much of the resilience, and most of the curiosity of Odysseus, as well as a number of minor traits but not, unfortunately, the verbal ingenuity. Bloom is not a gifted speaker. In a culture that values speech at times more than truth, he is denied eloquence. This is not to disagree with Richard Ellmann[3] and others who have emphasized Bloom's gift of expression or even his poetic diction. This diction, the remarkable crispness and spontaneity of his language, his certainly more than average wit, are confined to his unspoken thoughts. When lovable, adaptable, considerate, inquisitive Bloom opens his mouth and speaks aloud (what the Greeks called *aqoreusai,* as in *Od.* 5. 183), he may become a bit of a bore. At least that is how he strikes most of those who know him in Dublin (and the criteria applied throughout in this essay are of course mainly those of Bloom's fellow Dubliners and not some absolute standards of eloquence). Bloom knows it and is known for it. (You would not invite him to your party for the epigrammatic sparkle that he might provide.)

The brisk, supple commonsense of his many inner observations ("He boomed that workaday worker tack for all it was worth," 118, is a fair sample) rarely finds voice. With most of us Bloom shares the inhibitions that make us falter and grope for the clinching expression (which may be one of the reasons why it is so easy to empathize with him). He speaks as most of us do, haltingly. In the "Aeolus" chapter, which paradigmatically parades most rhetorical devices of the classical heritage, he comes out with a report like: "I spoke with Mr Keyes just now. . . . And he wants it if it's not too late I told councillor Nannetti from the *Kilkenny People*" (146). There is nothing wrong with that except some confusion and perhaps a certain lack of dramatic tension. This is how we conduct some of our daily conversation, but it is hardly the stuff that would make an irate, impatient, fidgety and, moreover thirsty, newspaperman hold his breath even if he were interested in the trivial business transaction. Mulligan would never speak like that.

Bloom's early morning classroom lecture about metempsychosis is faultless, and didactically sound, but it manifestly does not grip the attention of his audience of one. This is typical. Try to ask any reader of *Ulysses* if they remember what Bloom's first spoken words are, as they remember Mulligan's. Few of them do, and for good reason, for Bloom's opening line is singularly nonmemorable, a mere response to the cat's request (and significantly, Bloom tends to re-spond, re-ply, rather than initiate talk). What Bloom says is "O, there you are" (55).

The two openings of the novel contrast pointedly. Mulligan, from an elevated position, on top of an outstanding historical fortification, puts on an act, in a solemn voice, intoning, speaking up to *"Deus,"* though frivolously. Bloom, in the most commonplace of all rooms, a kitchen, from below ground level, speaks, in the most ordinary fashion, down to an animal, but without condescension. The unspectacular words are sufficient for the rapport with the cat that is needed. Note, incidentally, that Bloom begins his day by saying "you," while Mulligan starts out with "I" (*"Introibo"*) (3).

And, while on the subject of first words, we may observe that Stephen is first heard saying "Tell me" (4), which happens to coincide with the first words of the first line of the *Odyssey* in many translations.

With intimates like the cat or Molly or (for all we know) Milly, Bloom is still more at ease; with an old friend like Josie Breen he may even venture a flourish like "your lord and master" (157). Towards others he is more reserved. Approaching Larry O'Rourke, he rehearses a little speech which he then keeps for himself. He rarely tries to match the elocution of the Irishmen around him, but he admires them for their wit. Simon Dedalus is one of them: "Most amusing expressions that man finds. Hhhn: burst sidewise" (103). The Muse in general is reticent toward Bloom and does not inspire his expressions.

Surely a chapter like "Circe" gives evidence of Bloom's aspirations to be a great orator as well; he would enjoy swaying a large audience. In "Eumaeus," with some of the inhibitions gone, his submerged eloquence finds a belated outlet but also, tragically, only a completely unresponsive audience. On the whole Bloom is aware of his limits and rarely exceeds them without provocation. Lenehan recalls an occasion when Bloom was holding forth on a favorite subject, astronomy, at some length, but it is obvious that the attention of most of his listeners was elsewhere, and Lenehan ultimately turns the event into the kind of lively story that Bloom could never bring off (233–35). Bloom is at his best as a silent observer and internal commentator. Ironically, his job connects him with the "modern art of advertising," which depends so much on the catchy phrase that Bloom can judge but not make up. The ideal "of magnetising efficacy to arrest involuntary attention, to interest, to convince, to decide" (683) remains an ideal.

Of course Bloom is not at all inarticulate, he is simply not particularly eloquent; his talk, not very exciting, is still more interesting than that of some others. Early in the day he runs into one of the least inspired speakers, Charles M'Coy, who treats him to an unwelcome, protracted report on his response to the news of Dignam's death. This textbook illustration of narrative tedium (which Bloom, as far as Fate will allow him, relieves by voyeuristic attention) may indicate the lack of interest in news that the eating of the lotus fruit caused (*Od*. 9. 95), but it mainly shows that someone else is treated by Bloom as he often is by others. Marvin Magalaner long ago pointed out that M'Coy is Bloom's forerunner, an earlier version of him.[4] As M'Coy tries to wedge his way into the prestigious conversation of Cunningham & Co., he obliges, unbidden, with physiological terms of the Bloomian kind ("Mucus," "thorax," D 158) but remains neglected very much as Bloom will be in the same company in the funeral carriage.

The "Hades" chapter assesses Bloom's place in society. Attention rarely turns to him and, when it does, it is against his will. This happens when Molly's concert tour is mentioned, and again when his unorthodox remarks on death, in a different key from accepted ones, clash with the appropriate ritualized formulae (95). But he is ignored or thwarted when he wants to contribute to the conversation, when he volunteers his story about Reuben J. Dodd and son. There is, however, also good rhetorical reason for the usurpation of Bloom's tale. He gets off on a risky start by announcing, twice, how "awfully good" the story is, and only a skilled storyteller can live up to such a promise. When he settles down to the unmistakable tone which is required ("There was a girl in the case, . . . and he determined to send him to the Isle of Man out of harm's way . . ."), he is not too successful in keeping paternal and filial identities apart, and there are numerous interruptions for clarification until Cunningham takes the story away from him and presents a reedited, and superior, version which he insists on carrying to its climax. Clearly Bloom's narrative talent would not qualify him to negotiate "the funny part" (94–95).

As it happens, Bloom's story is launched just about when the carriage is closest to the newspaper offices off Sackville street. In general, Bloom stays away from the uncongenial role of a storyteller. The reader knows why in this case, after the sight of Blazes Boylan, and with a moneylender looming into view, he has deviated from his usual practice.

The episode in which Bloom fares best is the visual, projectional, reflective, and almost wordless scene on the beach. As a silent, dark, mysterious stranger he can appear attractive to a girl who is hesitant to move. He realizes that talk would not have improved the encounter. "Suppose I spoke to her. What about? Bad plan . . ." (370). He briefly considers gambits but shrewdly rejects them. A man like Boylan would not have any such qualms. A few sentences he throws out are enough to show that he hits upon the right tone with ease, in front of a shop girl or a barmaid. "What's the damage?" or "Why don't you grow" (227, 265) are not great aphorisms, but impressive enough to cause a blush or a sigh.

With his commonsense approach and his commonsense vocabulary, and some business to attend to, Bloom walks into the newspaper office where a rhetorical seminar is going on. For a moment he stops the stylistic analysis in progress by asking a few questions, short but to the point, "pertinent" (124) in fact. This word characterizes him, his speech and his acts; he "holds on to" whatever is at hand. His purposeful bearing and his simple statements set him off from the grandiose mannerisms of most others. His own words are trite, factual, polite, and unexciting. Yet his exit and his reappearance are decorated by theatrical gestures and elocutionary flourishes. As long as he remains peripheral he is treated with neglect, condescension, or mild ridicule, but as soon as he has to assert himself he becomes a nuisance.

Joyce chose the rhetorical setting of the "Aeolus" chapter, of all the possible settings, for a close-up view of Bloom in search of a pithy retort to Menton's recent snub. He moreover gives Bloom the advantage of a moment's unruffled leisure and the benefit of hindsight. If we try to imagine how some of the more sharp-tongued Dubliners would have reacted, or remember how Odysseus was able to epiphrase his myths with strategic cunning, we can appreciate the endearing flatfootedness of Bloom's effort:

I could have said when he clapped on his topper. . . . [No inspiration yet; the sting is slow in coming. So try again:] I ought to have said something about an old hat or something. No . . .

[Try once more:] I could have said. [The sentence without a pointed *mot* is still incomplete.] Looks as good as new now. [121]

As good as new? No "topper" is forthcoming, "old hat" is about right.

Cousin Bloom will never be an orator.[5] Nor, for that matter, was another figure who is featured, paradoxically, more in this chapter than in any other one. Moses—who also at times found it hard to get his people's attention—was "not eloquent . . . but I am slow of speech and of a slow tongue" (or ". . . *impeditioris et tardioris linguae sum,*" Exod. 4:10).[6]

To make up for a deficiency in brilliance, Bloom often has some pertinent factual information, for which, worse luck, there is not much of a market in his environment. One's reputation is based more on Aeolian lustre which, in the book, is glorified and mocked, but expansively displayed throughout. A later chapter will be devoted to the seduction (and the vacuity) of musical performances. "Sirens" through appropriate changes shapes words with regard to their sensuous appeal. Its overture is the most conspicuous example in the whole book of the celebration of pure aural entertainment, a matter of sound and phrasing and orchestration, an orgy of tonal rhetorics, before, secondarily, the sense can and will come through.

The music, to which Bloom listens, serves the same function to those present that talk does in "Cyclops"; it affords distraction. But in Barney Kiernan's pub Bloom imprudently tries to compete. Not a habitual pub-crawler, he is lured by circumstances and a specific invitation into the locality, and because of his displaced aggression the otherwise silent observer becomes unusually talkative. He behaves with oddly un-Odyssean rashness; he distinctly does not resort to "words of guile" or "deceit" (as in *Od. 9. 282*), but appears naively truthful and accurate in what he says and at times unnecessarily officious and intrusive, which aggravates his already precarious situation.

"Cyclops," one of the gregarious chapters, develops traits and themes from "Aeolus": coming and going, rambling and interrupted dialogue, discussion and parody of newspaper mannerisms, narrative disruptions, a shared cast (Lenehan, Lambert, O'Molloy, Hynes), and the application of oratory—a reasonably comprehensive list of rhetorical forms could be gleaned from this chapter too.[7] Again we have a group of some expert talkers and a few expert critics. The Citizen excels in one kind of invective and takes the opportunity to address the public in several set speeches.[8] Even the dog Garryowen holds the stage for a spell of cynical oratory. Bloom inadvertently maneuvers himself into the position of a public speaker. He is not comfortable in the role and breaks off his proclamation of love in a somewhat abrupt manner, obviously sensing that the audience is not quite with him. The scene is set for his second speech towards the end of the chapter, with the externals of a temporary rostrum and an expectant gathering. Rhetorical repetition characterizes Bloom's parting words (342) which clearly have a kinetic effect, but again this is not the occasion for a grandiose peroration. The burst of forensic eloquence is exceptional for Bloom (it becomes the rule in "Circe," but "Cyclops" serves in many ways as a rehearsal for the later chapter), and remains a qualified success. The reader knows what unusual provocation has led to this singular tortuous climax.

All along in the chapter, Bloom has been a multiple transgressor. It is not his own fault, nor even quite strictly true, that ethnically he does not really belong to the group. He might know, however, that to avoid being treated and treating again is not good policy (though others manage to get around this one with impunity). But beyond all that, Bloom proceeds in the wrong conversational key. He informs and instructs, or argues, or voices *his* grievances—but he does not amuse. There is a tacit code that Bloom seems (or chooses) to be unaware of. The prevalence of such codes is signaled early on in an act put on between the Citizen and Joe Hynes when

they go through the ritual of the passwords of the Ribbonmen, with all the required gestures (295),[9] as if to indicate
some of the rules of the game.

There are other violators present. Bob Doran, who bears
his own understandable grudge against providence, irately
seizes upon the literal sense of the word "good" in relation to
Christ and Dignam's death and is instantly admonished—
"they didn't want that kind of talk in a respectable licensed
premises" (302). There are indeed "premises" that one had
better observe. Remarks about the responsibilities or the
ethnic background of divinity are clearly taboo, even if other
blasphemies may be cheerfully applauded. Fittingly, an earlier verbal transgression of Bloom is worked into this chapter,
his "giving lip to a grazier" (315). This observance of his own
personal code above the socially accepted one led to his
dismissal from a job.

The tacit rules are simple enough. You keep the party going
by being wittily entertaining (which may amount to finding
new permutations for old jocularities), and you play straight
man to the Citizen and prompt him to his histrionics (though
you may laugh behind his back). But you do not seriously
argue or waste everybody's good time with explanations or
technicalities. To define a nation, or love, or injustice, just
does not make you popular. Who cares, anyway, about
mortgages, insurance, or hoose drench?—except perhaps
widows or cattle, but none of those are present. The nameless
narrator is irritated by Bloom as he is also once by J. J.
O'Molloy when he helps out with some legal point about the
laws of libel: "Who wants your opinion? Let us drink our
pints in peace," as though mere factual clarification were
somehow to disturb that peace (321).

Bloom is a disturbance, and part of it is due to the sense
that he has little value as an entertainer. His inauguration
speech is exemplary. The floor at the moment is being held by
Alf Bergan, one of Dublin's wits and one thoroughly familiar
with the ground rules (he may break some other ones; surely

the public reading of the letters received from hangmen is
hardly professional etiquette for a civil servant—but the
letters *are* amusing). He offers a report on naive Denis Breen
as a diversion (Breen, taunted by the verbal insult "U.p.: up,"
promptly tries to bring a gravely different code, the legal one,
to bear upon what has been designed only "for a lark" (299).
Bergan appears impatient with serious talk about capital
punishment and uses (what is no doubt Bloom's phrase)
"deterrent effect" to broach the much more fascinating topic
of the erection of a hanged man (304). To this there are, in
neat instructive juxtaposition, two responses. The one,
entirely in the spirit of the game, by Joe Hynes:

—Ruling passion strong in death, . . . as someone said

is a maliciously clever shift of a well-known line to a new,
amusing context. The deviant response is, naturally, Bloom's

—That can be explained by science. . . . It's only a natural
phenomenon, don't you see, because on account of the . . . [304]

We, the readers, can see how Bloom does not want to have
the talk turn around erection at this particular moment, but
scientific explanation has a way of spoiling the fun. Accounts
are the last thing wanted, and Bloom's speech is, once more,
rudely thwarted, this time by the narrator who instantly
substitutes a commentary on Bloom for Bloom's verbatim
lecture. And a parodistic interpolation follows right away in
which Bloom's characteristic approach and his interest in
medical evidence are satirized. Bloom has started on the
wrong foot, he comes out "with the why and the wherefore
and all the codology of the business" (304). He wants to argue
and only provokes arguments *ad hominem* and quips at his
expense, often with anti-Semitic overtones—"Professor Luit-
pold Blumenduft" (304).
  The scientist Bloom, "Mister Knowall" (315), with his

useful though tedious contributions about sheep-dip, rower's heart, discipline, insurance or persecution, is out of place, "putting in his old goo" (310–11), "mucking it up" (313), a nuisance even if he had not mentioned, of all things, "the antitreating league" (311)—a rhetorical exile as well. One of his favorite phrases is "as a matter of fact" when facts are the least interesting things anyone wants to hear. He may well be right about the racial origin of Marx or Spinoza,[10] or even the Saviour, but such information would fail to rouse much interest at the best of times and, at this juncture, merely reinforces the prejudices against him. It matters very little that the Citizen and his faction are contradictory and inconsistent. For all the proximity of the courts and the thematic relevance of parliament and debates at the meetings about the Irish language or the cattle traders, no one wants an objective debate with pro and con. This is a gathering for having "a great confab," as we are warned early on (295), for drolleries like "don't cast your nasturtiums" (320), for clever impersonations ("taking off the old recorder," 322), where forms of "codding" are the order of the day, or "letting on" is expected as well as variations of "doing the repparee" (295), ". . . the weeps" (302), ". . . the mollycoddle" (306), etc. Rhetorical compulsion requires the translation of Bloom's straightforward "cigar" into the code expression "Give us one of your prime stinkers," or at least some minor elaboration like "knockmedown cigar" (304, 305). This minor incident of Hynes forcing a cigar on reluctant Bloom is transformed by the narrator into "his twopenny stump that he cadged off Joe" (311), a bit of a distortion and a slightly more diverting story. Occasionally clarity demands the reverse translation from the coded allusion to normal terminology. "Wine of the country" and "Ditto MacAnaspey" are put into the vernacular—"Three pints" (295). We learn that "Half one . . . and a hands up" amounts to "Small whisky and bottle of Allsop" (328).[11] Such terminological shifts within the dialogue are in realistic analogy, on a small scale, to the major stylistic and perspectival transitions of the later chapters and of *Ulysses* as a whole.

Where everybody is expected to wield tropes divertingly, for the fun of it, Bloom remains, even in his most rhetorical moments, factual (whether he gets the facts right or not), sincere and truthful, devoid of Odyssean trickery. The "Cyclops" chapter exemplifies the free transposition of Homeric material, the diversified distribution of epic roles, and it shows that many of the ill-termed "parallels" are not in fact parallel, but often inverted. Homer's episode confronts the civilized Greeks with uncouth and lawless giants who rely on their muscular strength. Much of this is transferred straight. Humane Bloom is holding his own against opponents who are biased, prejudiced, or brutal. And yet it is also Bloom who does not abide by the laws of the place, and he is even, according to the criteria of the regular customers, a barbarian—he speaks a strange and different language, is not conversant with the rules and yet still speaks out. He is a spoilsport, a disquieting intruder.

Imprudently (and the reader knows why), he talks more than normally. This makes him, in an odd doubling of roles, also a Polyphemus, literally *poly-phemos*, from *pheme* (in turn derived from *phemi*, I speak; cognate with Latin *fama* and "famous"): voice, speech, word, report, renown—and rumor. In fact the whole chapter is *polyphemos*, full of voices, talk, resounding exaggeration, and rumor—with an empty biscuit tin thrown in for bad measure. Conversely, it is as though this episode of elaborate naming were also to utilize the only etymology of the name Odysseus in the whole poem: it connects him with *odyssamenos* (*Od.* 19. 407), the participle of a verb "to be angry" ("in great wrath," Butcher and Lang). A surprising number of participants are in fact angry about one thing or another, starting with the narrator, the debtor Geraghty and his contestant Herzog—"the little jewy getting his shirt out" (292), and on to Denis Breen, Bob Doran, Bloom, Garryowen, and the Citizen. Anger lends force to Bloom's two outbursts and his subliminal belligerence. "Cyclops" is suffused with "suppressed rancour" (312).

Straightforward Bloom is distrusted, but Lenehan (both glibly *polyphemos* and angrily *odyssamenos* about his gambling losses), whose sayings at all times would merit the least literal credibility, is believed immediately when he suspects Bloom to be the only man in Dublin to have won money by backing Throwaway. The reader knows that this *fama* primordially derives from Bantam Lyons projecting onto nongambling Bloom a rhetorical and allusive ingenuity which he neither has nor ever attempts. But it may well be Bloom's factual bias which makes it easier for the others to believe that he may have had some inside knowledge, or to believe the other rumor attached to him, that he "gave the idea for Sinn Fein to Griffith" (335): he might well be the sort of person who would help the cause with pertinent specific advice. But not even that momentary patriotic halo bestowed upon Bloom by a tenuous political connection would make him any more popular.

Another interesting quasi-political parallel was pointed out to me by Wayne Hall.[12] The absent hero Charles Stewart Parnell was not a gifted speaker either, and in his early parliamentary appearances even a notably poor one, and he had at times a stammer. This un-Irish deficiency might have contributed to his cultivation of a pose of taciturnity and aloofness, a manner which would have stood Bloom in good stead when facing Parnell's talkative epigones.

Bloom's talk, for reasons mentioned, is often cut short by the others, or else the narrator simply ignores the talk and replaces it with his own more racy paraphrases. In the narrator's opinion, Bloom would, and does, talk at length and "talk steady," monotonously so.

In the long run, this might well pall on the reader too. So, following the precedent of the nameless narrator of "Cyclops," Joyce from now on does not allow Bloom—or anyone else, for that matter—to "talk steady" *in his own spoken*

words. Instead he takes over more and more. The daytalk of
Ulysses culminates in Barney Kiernan's noisy pub and then
gives way to nocturnal transformations. Bloom's unappreciated miniloquence has been sufficiently established and
needs no further illustration. But the novel itself becomes
more and more extravagantly multiloquent; it begins to
change its voices away from actual speech, even though the
voices still remain a substratum which can be, on demand,
dexterously extrapolated.

Direct transmission of spoken words after "Cyclops" becomes the exception. What is being said is translated,
metempsychosed, reflected (refracted is it?) into new variations and stranger modes.

"Nausicaa" contains some vestiges of dialogue, but is
essentially silent and/or stylized according to its own laws.
There is just one indirect speech by Bloom. Since his watch is
not functioning at this point he cannot even do what he is best
at, give accurate information, and so has to fall back on
circumstantial evidence. Again the reader knows that Bloom's
small audience does not really care about the information in
the first place. Gerty MacDowell registers mainly the "cul-
tured ring" and the "measured accents" (361). Cissy Caffrey,
the most linguistically venturesome girl of the group
("jaspberry ram," 353), does just what Joyce has been doing,
she gives Bloom's words a narrative touch, in a different key:
"uncle said his waterworks were out of order" (361).

In "Oxen of the Sun" dialogue surfaces only rarely verbatim, if at all, and is mainly refined into various literary
impersonations. Only the last pages of the chapter look like a
return to actual speech faithfully recorded (as if by a tape
recorder), as though it were the real performance of a sur-
prisingly articulate group of *ad hoc* orators. But we are not
quite sure if this placental verbiage is meant to be the substance of what the students are really saying in precisely these
words, in precisely those roles, or whether these spurts of
instant ingenuity may not also be tampered with by a more

and more manipulative author. Even if the talk is just talk, it is of the kind that Mulligan, for one, can command, and not of the Bloomian variety. One might indeed describe the second part of *Ulysses*—all those chapters, that is, that do not conform to S. L. Goldberg's aesthetic dogmas[13]—as a taking over of the Mulliganesque features which prevailed in "Telemachus."

In "Circe" dialogue is ubiquitous but only part of it is actually real and spoken aloud. And there is no way of dispelling doubt that anything in it might not be imaginary or at least metamorphosed by the governing magic. By now all appearances have become frankly deceptive.

Of the *Nostos* chapters, only "Eumaeus" reinstates direct speech, and plenty of it; it is a return to ground which is familiar. Bloom finally takes the opportunity to hold forth at great length, in compensation for all that has gone before. He pulls out all the stops and becomes rhetorically over-ambitious; he is figurative and metaphorical and engages in elegant variations—all to no avail, of course, as Stephen is only minimally interested in what Bloom says and not at all in the way he says it. But again, does Bloom really and extend-edly speak like that, *verbatim*? Are the following Bloom's actual words, faithfully transcribed:

> —Spaniards, for instance, . . . passionate temperaments like that, impetuous as Old Nick, are given to taking the law into their own hands and give you your quietus double quick with those poignards they carry in the abdomen. [637]

There are his idioms, his recognizable cadences, and yet his diction, especially in this relentlessly concentrated form, may be tarred with the brush that is responsible for the stylistic idiosyncrasies of the whole chapter, which of course, in turn, merely exaggerate the potential of his own mind. Perhaps it just no longer makes sense to distinguish actual performance from what are no doubt oratorical aspirations and those, in turn, from the mode of the chapter. *Ulysses* also teaches us to let go—reluctantly, at times—some of those neat categories that our minds have been brought up on. In practical terms this might mean that, at this late stage, we may not even trust the dashes any longer, that typographical convention by which, so far, direct speech was honestly set off from the rest of the narration. Sounds and speeches and dashes may be impostures in "Eumaeus," a chapter of guises and subterfuges.

Clearly, both "Circe" and "Eumaeus," in their own particular modes, hint at a distorted fulfillment of Bloom's rhetorical (and authorial) aspirations, as if in compensation for what he cannot bring off in his actual day by day performances. Yet in both chapters of wishful triumphs, Bloom's fumbles and blunders too are magnified correspondingly and grotesquely.

And again, it seems that Joyce removes the novel at this point from even these highly hypothetical excrescencies of Bloomian ambitions with their semblance of direct quotation. In "Ithaca" direct speech has disappeared entirely and given way to pointedly oblique report, which is catalogued dead pan along with everything else, though we can, of course, try to reconstruct Bloom's and Stephen's actual spoken words by an empirical, inductive process.

The Peneloquence of the last chapter is unspoken, though based on spoken language, and *sui generis*. It does, however, reintroduce some of Bloom's sentences to Molly, spoken with effect and remembered with relish. Bloom undoubtedly is capable, at times. Even so, without the setting of rhododendrons and romantic wooing, "the sun shines for you" and you are "a flower of the mountain" (782) are not necessarily, by themselves, evidence of remarkable rhetorical potential.

In grammatical metaphor, Bloom's progress through his fourteen chapters is from the predominant indicative mood (corresponding to his acts, thoughts, and talk) into different moods like subjunctive or optative, expressing more the

aspirations, imaginatory achievements, fears or wishful
thinking. Much of "Circe" is written in a kind of conditional:
if Bloom could get up for a stump speech, and *if* he could
conjure up the right phrases on the spur of the moment, and *if*
. . . , then he might undergo such rapid changes and rise to
glory and also suffer such ignominies. And if he had the
resources of a Mr. Philip Beaufoy (or, as he seems to think, of
Stephen Dedalus, poet and man of letters), then he might be
able to compose such figurative, parabolic, ornate, winged,
fumbling, discordant, and alert (yes, alert) prose as the one of
"Eumaeus."

The rhetorics and tropes which Bloom lacks in everyday
life are lavished on the novel as a novel, with increasing
boldness. The book as an event in language plays most of the
roles, along with, and above, the characters. The smooth and
sweet and cunning words that Odysseus contrives when he
first addresses Nausicaa (*Od.* 6. 143 ff.) are never even attempted by Bloom, but they inform the first part of the softly
featured and mellifluent chapter. Beyond the reaches of any
one person, the book becomes mercurial, myriadminded,
multifaceted, histrionic, and polytropically all-round.

The mind around which all this mainly revolves is, like
most minds, relatively pedestrian. Mr. Bloom's own utterances can be improved upon by a good translation. So Joyce
comes to his aid and more and more conspicuously runs the
show on his behalf, with transformations, transmutations,
transubstantiations, and metamorphoses, with different con-
texts and styles and parallactic systems of correspondences. It
did not occur to the detractors of *Ulysses* that even its more
elaborate features, whatever else, also work against the boredom of anything that is carried on for too long. That is all
done with a purpose and with consideration for the reader,
believe it or not, "to cheer a fellow up" (107).

Joyce puts poor Bloom, who endures many troubles and
hardships (*Od.* 1. 4), at one of the greatest further disadvan-
tages, by depriving him of a quality that Homer, the Greeks,

the Irish, and most lovers of literature and talk, value highly. But he lends him his sympathy, does duty as his own personal Muse and gives assistance by metaphrasing more and more of his words and by providing him (though Bloom would never know)—and us (and we had better know it)—with a course in remedial rhetorics.

NOTES

1. *Ulysses* is quoted according to the edition by Random House, New York, 1961. Numbers in parenthesis refer to the pagination of this edition. For *Dubliners* (*D* + page number) and *A Portrait of the Artist as a Young Man* (*P* + page number) the texts of the Viking Critical Library, The Viking Press, New York, 1969 and 1968, are used.

2. "*Polytropos*, he [Antisthenes] argues, does not refer to character or ethics at all. It simply denotes Odysseus's skill in adapting his figures of speech ('tropes') to his hearers at any particular time." In W. B. Stanford, *The Ulysses Theme: A Study in the Adaptability of a Traditional Hero*, 2d ed. (Ann Arbor: University of Michigan Press, 1968), p. 99. See Fritz Senn, "Odysseeische Metamorphosen," in *James Joyce's "Ulysses": Neuere deutsche Aufsätze*, ed. Therese Fischer-Seidel (Frankfurt: edition Suhrkamp, 1977), p. 44; and Michael Groden, *"Ulysses" in Progress* (Princeton, N. J.: Princeton University Press, 1977), pp. 91–92.

3. "Yet [Bloom] must be separated from those about him, and by the gift of expression—the highest a writer can bestow on his creature. . . . But Bloom has to speak in ordinary language . . . taking a keen pleasure in manoeuvring among common idioms, allusions, and proverbs. It is this power of speech, mostly inward speech, that inclines Bloom towards Odysseus." In Richard Ellmann, *Ulysses on the Liffey* (London: Faber and Faber, 1972), p. 30.

4. Marvin Magalaner, "Leopold Bloom Before *Ulysses*," *Modern Language Notes* 68 (February 1953): 110–12.

5. But then, Bloom's first words spoken in "Aeolus" constitute the best all-time editorial advice that fits all occasions: "Just cut it out" (116).

6. The implication is that eloquence is not everything, and anyway, the Lord said, "Who hath made man's mouth" (Exod. 4:11). Intriguingly, Stephen, who has worked "mouth" into the semiplagiarized creation recalled in the chapter, speculates at length on the reverberations of this word. "Must be some" (138).

7. See also Phillip F. Herring, ed., *Joyce's Notes and Early Drafts for "Ulysses": Selections from the Buffalo Collection* (Charlottesville, Va.: University Press of Virginia, 1977), p. 146; and Groden, *"Ulysses" in Progress*, p. 133 ff. To all these lists might be added the parallel that in both chapters Bloom appears twice and on his return gets worse treatment each time.

8. The Citizen's "No music and no art and no literature worthy of the name" (325) follows, roughly, a pattern set in Taylor's speech (142).

9. Hugh B. Staples, " 'Ribbonmen' Signs and Passwords in *Ulysses*," *Notes and Queries*, n.s. 13 (1966): 95–96.

10. In the roll call of great Jews in Bloom's enumeration (342), Mercadante is the odd one out, by no stretch of ethnic definition a Jew. What happened is that Bloom has been confusing two composers he likes for different reasons, Mercadante (82) and Meyerbeer (168). In "Sirens" he wrongly attributed *Seven Last Words* to Meyerbeer (290) and now, in his unrehearsed speech, seems to make up for it. He means Meyerbeer, whose opera *The Huguenots* is about religious persecution.

11. It is important to have no misunderstanding interfere with the order of one's drink, but these variations also comply to the avoidance of mere repetition in conventional rhetorics.

12. A former student at Indiana University who mentioned this when an earlier version of this essay was presented as a talk.

13. S. L. Goldberg, *The Classical Temper: A Study of James Joyce's "Ulysses"* (London: Chatto and Windus, 1961); to this day still the best book ever written against *Ulysses*.